THIS BOOK BELONGS

GORDON DONAHYE

ROUTE #003
STOCK TRANSPORTATION

RETURN TO ME
A. S. A. P
THANKS

HOME → 905 - ~~597~~ 597 - 5720

CELL → 416 803 - 7225

ALSO BY JOSHUA KNELMAN

Hot Art: Chasing Thieves and Detectives through the Secret World of Stolen Art

Four Letter Word: New Love Letters (edited by Joshua Knelman and Rosalind Porter)

FIREBRAND

A Tobacco Lawyer's Journey

ALLEN
LANE

Joshua Knelman

ALLEN LANE

an imprint of Penguin Canada, a division of Penguin Random House Canada Limited

Canada • USA • UK • Ireland • Australia • New Zealand • India • South Africa • China

First published 2022

www.penguinrandomhouse.ca

LIBRARY AND ARCHIVES CANADA CATALOGUING IN PUBLICATION

Title: Firebrand : a tobacco lawyer's journey / Joshua Knelman.
Names: Knelman, Joshua, author.
Identifiers: Canadiana (print) 20220142238 | Canadiana (ebook) 20220150508 |
    ISBN 9780735243811 (hardcover) | ISBN 9780735243828 (EPUB)
Subjects: LCSH: Cigarette industry. | LCSH: Tobacco industry. | LCSH: Cigarette industry—
    Moral and ethical aspects. | LCSH: Tobacco industry—Moral and ethical aspects. |
    LCSH: Social responsibility of business. | LCSH: Corporate lawyers—Biography.
Classification: LCC HD9149.C42 K64 2022 | DDC 381/.4567973—dc23

Book design by Matthew Flute
Cover design by Dylan Browne
Cover image: (Hand holding cigarette) © CSA-Printstock / Getty Images

Printed in Canada

10 9 8 7 6 5 4 3 2 1

Penguin
Random
House

"Illusion is the first of all pleasures."

—VOLTAIRE

For Judith Knelman and Sylvia Ostry—wise ones

AUTHOR'S NOTE

This is a selfish book.

For some readers, it may hold value as an exploration of the contemporary tobacco industry, a crash course in global marketing, or a primer on multinational business careers—after all, this story spans more than a dozen countries. Other curious souls may simply appreciate a passport stamped with so much ink.

I wrote it, though, because I'm a smoker, and I got hooked on this international adventure connected to the most contentious and dangerous mass market consumer product in the history of the world.

Over a drink at a bar, I first met the man at the centre of this narrative, who worked in the tobacco industry as legal counsel for over a decade and for a variety of multinational companies. He was engaging and a gifted storyteller—I was drawn in, and inhaled the information and the intelligence being offered. Despite years of repelling sustained attacks, he pointed out, the tobacco industry was thriving.

After that first conversation, I was struck by how little I knew about the product to which I had become addicted—and my curiosity was stoked by a burning question. So I asked for a second meeting and posed it: How had an entire globalized industry managed to survive decades of intense and sustained assault by the medical and scientific establishment, and from governments around the world, while keeping its product on the shelf? He nodded and smiled: "That's the trillion-dollar-question, isn't it? I can do my best to explain it to you." Our interviews took place over the next ten years.

It felt distinctly absurd to gain more and more knowledge about this popular and deadly consumer product from someone who had helped market it to the world even as I bought and used it daily, struggling with my ferocious addiction.

I hope you enjoy reading about the tobacco paradox taking place across our globe as much as I enjoyed listening and learning about it. Names have been changed, but the truth remains. As someone who has smoked tens of thousands of cigarettes, I wanted, it turned out, to know more about the thing that may kill me. Who wouldn't, I guess?

—J.K., Toronto, 2022

INTERVIEWS

Until the age of eleven, he wanted to be a pirate. Then he decided he wanted to be the next Johnny Carson.

So he chased a job working for NBC—Johnny's network—and got one in its news department in the UK. Just a few months into it, though, he realized he'd never make any money at journalism. So he applied to law school.

Well, *applied* is a loose term. It was his father who provided the strategy: go inquire at the most prestigious schools and find out if any prospective students had dropped out. He followed his dad's advice, visited admissions offices across London, and got lucky. At one law school, the secretary asked him about grades, and, of course, he'd brought his transcript. She examined the documents, looked at him, and said if he could pay a deposit by the end of day, the spot was his.

He paid and gained entrance to one of the best law schools in Britain. For two years he worked his ass off, and at the end of it he passed his law finals.

In the UK, becoming a lawyer is not exactly like it is in the US or in Canada, where he'd grown up. In Britain, you went to university, you went to law school, you took your bar exams, and then you had to work two years as an apprentice. You then became a solicitor —and a few years after that, you could practise on your own. Since the intake of lawyers was completely determined by the private sector, a lot of people who went to law school never actually became lawyers. There were simply not enough positions.

Luck was with him again when he graduated: he was recruited as one of only two new lawyers by an entertainment law firm. Even better, their offices weren't in a corporate tower but in a renovated fashion district warehouse. Serendipity: he got the job not only because he had attended an excellent school but also, he thinks, because he'd worked as a journalist with NBC. The journalism experience gave his resumé some edge.

It was 1998, and this second millennium seemed to close in his favour. At twenty-four years old, he had a law degree and a starter career at a boutique law outfit. It was the stuff of dreams. The only problem: everyone else at the new firm seemed cool, and he was not.

This sad fact was reflected in his new responsibilities. He was immediately assigned to all the un-cool work: advertising, trademarks, branding—the boring stuff. He didn't get his own office. Instead, he shared a room with someone more attractive than he was and who worked on more exciting files. Her name was Leah. Talk about cool. Leah was stunning, tall, intense, and her boyfriend was a famous DJ on the club-music scene. They were making plans to get married at a castle in Italy.

He had a fiancée, whom he was crazy about, but they were not considering European castles for their wedding.

He and Leah clicked, thank god—in fact, they'd met at law school —because the space they co-occupied was tiny. Leah respected him for his intelligence, he supposed. He respected her because she was super-hip, and he hoped that by working in such close proximity to one another, some of her coolness would transfer to him by osmosis.

For almost three years, he worked out of that compact office with his beautiful and talented co-worker. Back then, he wasn't issued a computer; he was provided with a Dictaphone. He focused on contractual and intellectual property matters and was expected to attend a lot of entertainment events in smoke-filled nightclubs. He didn't like nightclubs, but he did like smoking.

One afternoon, he received a phone call from a recruitment agent—a headhunter.

"Are you interested in an in-house legal position for a large multi-national?" she asked him.

The headhunter said she could not identify, at this time, the name of the multinational, so, naturally, he was immediately interested.

After he hung up, he discussed the opportunity with Leah in their cramped office.

They envisaged a job working for

(a) an oil company, or
(b) a pornographic magazine empire.

Leah told him he'd be fantastic in either role. She was supportive.

He'd scribbled down an address from the headhunter, and a couple of days later he went to meet her during his lunch hour.

The address was at a large office building in Central London, in the City. He took a black cab from the hip office in the fashion district to the bespoke-suited hub of the business world. On the way to the interview, he was anything but nervous. He wasn't actively looking for work, after all, and he hadn't applied for the job.

The meeting, it turned out, was relatively casual.

Let's call the headhunter Heather.

Heather was a sleek and suited City woman. She was in her late twenties or early thirties, serious-minded, with large blue eyes and shampoo-commercial blond hair that was precision trimmed. She embodied the cunning corporate look in every detail: pencil skirt and a pale-blue Ralph Lauren shirt that brought out the blue in her eyes.

When she first looked at him, he had the feeling of being appraised, as a commodity. He was, in fact, her commodity. Their conversation felt clinical, like a doctor asking him to take his clothes off, and then prodding.

"Come in," she smiled. "Let's talk about this."

Heather placed two glasses of ice water on the table. He was struck by the way she sipped water throughout the meeting—the motion of her mouth as she quietly emptied the cold liquid from the glass. He felt like he'd entered an icy world. She had a list of questions and opened with a personal inquiry.

"Whom did you vote for in the last election?"

Tony Blair had recently swept to power and hammered the Conservatives.

He told Heather whom he had voted for.

"Would you have a problem working in an industry which people around you were critical of?"

He asked Heather for an example.

"For example, an oil company."

"I don't think so. I don't really know," he said.

So it was an oil company.

Heather asked him about his nationality.

He told her he was born in Canada.

She asked him about his visa status.

He explained that he was a British citizen, so that was not an issue.

Heather didn't seem particularly enthusiastic about any of his answers, even as she jotted everything neatly in a small notebook. The question period lasted for about twenty minutes, and no matter the answers he provided, she did not seem pleased or displeased. He noticed she did not ask a single question about his skills as a lawyer, which he found odd.

"We'll be in touch," she said, when the interview was over.

"Thank you," he said.

He took a black cab back to his law firm.

Leah was at her desk, waiting. He spent a few minutes downloading his experience, telling her that he thought it was an oil company, and that the meeting, overall, was a bizarre experience.

While he was talking to Leah, his phone rang. It was Heather.

She sounded slightly friendlier now. She addressed him by his first name and invited him back for a second interview, providing a choice of dates.

He picked the latest one, because work was busy; he was spending a lot of time on a client at the European patent office in Munich. It was a barrel of laughs. FYI: patent attorneys are people who find accounting too stimulating.

After they agreed on a date, Heather told him that at this second interview a senior lawyer from the company in question would be present. When he hung up, he reminded himself that he was gainfully employed at a super-cool law firm.

Leah looked at him, feigning hurt, and said, "You're going to get this job, aren't you . . ."

"I don't even know what this job is," he said.

Leah made a pout. "You're going to leave me here."

Two weeks later, he took a black cab back into the City.

This time, Ms. Ice Water greeted him warmly. It was almost as if she were performing for the benefit of the person joining them— her customer. The lawyer from the mystery multinational company was not posh. She was quite un-Heather, with less pretension and less-styled hair. Also, unlike Heather, she seemed extremely warm and genuinely friendly, right from "hello." She possessed an honest, maternal quality that made him feel at ease. Let's call her Mary.

The three of them sat down at the same small table, with three glasses of ice water.

Heather didn't waste any time. She began with a new round of questions.

"What would you do if you were asked by an employee to pay a bribe or make an untrue statement?"

"Well, I don't pay bribes," he answered. "And I won't make untrue statements. I take my professional status as a lawyer—and duties to the court—extremely seriously."

Heather looked at him, looked at her client, and nodded.

"That's the right answer," she assured him.

More ethics-based questions followed, and Heather jotted his answers down in her notebook.

Then the lawyer from the multinational asked him a question.

"Have you heard of _____?"

"No," he answered.

"Most people haven't," Mary said. "We make _____ cigarettes. Have you heard of them?"

"Yes."

Then Mary said her company wanted to hire a lawyer at their UK offices to work on international brand protection and to manage their sports sponsorships, as well as legal issues for their domestic UK market. Now he understood why the headhunter had called on him. At the entertainment firm, he was dealing with advertising and sponsorship work. So this was one hidden benefit of spending all those nights in smoky nightclubs.

The interview was shorter than he expected, and they still hadn't discussed anything relating to his skills as a lawyer or, he realized, his views on tobacco.

He left the meeting and met Leah for lunch. He told her all about the latest episode of his bizarre corporate adventure.

After lunch, his cell phone rang. Back in those days, cell phones were quite large; it didn't fit in his pocket. It was Heather. She asked what he thought of the interview.

He told her he thought it was quite positive.

Heather agreed and invited him to a third interview. This one would take place at the multinational's corporate headquarters, in about a week's time. He agreed.

In advance of that meeting, he tried to do some research about the company but couldn't find much information. There was no corporate website. For such a large, and apparently profitable, company, it seemed to keep a low profile—at least in terms of information available to the public.

Their HQ was a short drive outside of London.

When he arrived, he was taken into a meeting room with a lot of advertising paraphernalia on the walls. In the middle of the boardroom table was a big bowl filled with packs of cigarettes, unopened. He made the decision not to smoke.

Finally, he was asked questions about his legal experience and professional skills. His interviewers seemed satisfied. Their last question was this: "What is your greatest achievement to date?"

He went through a mental checklist and found the answer he knew was right.

"Meeting my beautiful fiancée, whom I'm about to marry in four months' time."

They thanked him for coming to the interview.

He'd barely driven out of the corporate compound when Heather called again. She wanted to know what he thought about the meeting.

He said the same as before: it was positive.

She agreed. That was all.

He didn't hear anything the next day.

The day after, Heather called and invited him to a fourth interview, in the private dining room at the corporate compound, to meet a group from the legal team.

He said yes.

Over lunch, he was introduced to some of the UK legal team. The menu was sandwiches cut into little triangles — smoked salmon, cucumber, egg mayonnaise, tuna — sausage rolls, Boddingtons beer, white wine, and tea.

He was slightly disoriented; the occasion felt more like an intimate party than a job interview. He was asked if he wanted to smoke. A few of the lawyers at the lunch were smoking. He had held off in the previous interviews, but now he joined in.

It was a warm group, and he was treated as one of them, even though no business was discussed. Without exception they all seemed like very nice, upper-middle-class, family oriented people. Everyone was relaxed.

After lunch, Mary asked him to join her for a tour.

She led him out of the private dining room and down a series of hallways to an open door. They looked into a spacious room with large windows with a view out to trees and sky. There was a desk with an expensive office chair and a high-end laptop. The laptop was becoming a necessity, because of a new trend in business communications: email. Other furnishings: a cupboard, credenza, and a meeting table. Two or three ornate ashtrays punctuated the desk and meeting table. It was the opposite of the cramped space he currently worked from.

"This would be your office," Mary said.

He had still not been offered a job.

On the drive back to London, the phone rang.

It was Heather — and she offered him the job.

———

The money was more than he was making at the entertainment firm. There was bonus potential, company share options, an incredible health care package, a gym membership, and—the best part —a company car. He'd been driving a beat-up Nissan Micra, a glorified golf cart. He often told people it was like driving a vacuum cleaner.

This time he did not brief Leah. When he arrived home that evening, he and his fiancée had a long conversation, and they were in agreement: this offer was a step towards the life they wanted to build together.

The next day at the law firm, as promised, he received a package from the multinational tobacco company. There was no company name on the envelope, and he waited until Leah left to open it. Inside was his letter of offer, some company policy material, a health questionnaire, and various documents related to which company car he needed to choose.

He had only one hesitation about accepting the job, and it wasn't ethical—it was around timing.

He called Mary and explained that he wanted to take the job but was getting married in a matter of weeks and was committed to his marriage and honeymoon plans.

Mary didn't even pretend that she had to ask the company; she immediately said it would be no problem at all. It was clear they wanted him. He telephoned the recruitment agent the next day and accepted the offer. He never spoke with Heather again.

To his surprise, the entertainment firm counter-offered.

That made him feel special, but he didn't consider the offer for a minute. It was a combination of factors. He liked the idea of joining a company rather than recording every minute of every day in a ledger. He liked that he was going to have his own office, his own company car, his own secretary, and would be working in an industry that was changing and challenging. From a lawyer's perspective, this new job was thrilling.

There was also the location. The company headquarters was on a beautiful compound, a vast tract of land with a forest. He wouldn't be getting on the Underground every morning. Instead, he'd be getting in his company car, driving against traffic, and pulling into a private parking space.

This was a step up, regardless of what money was being offered.

Leah was devastated, or at least she feigned it.

He left the entertainment firm, and within days he and his fiancée travelled to a magical castle in Tuscany for Leah's wedding.

The man Leah was marrying was not only a DJ but also the owner of a music label. The lawyer didn't fit in with any other guests, and he didn't keep up with the music scene, so he had no idea who these guys were. He found out later that a lot of them were UK music superstars.

He always got up early to smoke, and did so on the morning of the wedding. He went for breakfast at the castle's restaurant, and there, sitting at a table, were two DJs. He asked them if he could sit with them.

Sure, one of them said.

He told them, or confessed, that he didn't know a lot about dance music.

One of them asked him what he did for a living.

Without hesitation, he said he used to work with the bride-to-be at the entertainment firm but was now working as a tobacco lawyer.

The DJs were intrigued, and as they all smoked, they started asking more questions.

With no media training, and without having worked a single day at the company, he started talking about being a tobacco lawyer as if he already was one. What came over him? He has no idea, but he started talking about issues related to cancer and the fierce attacks focused on the industry he was joining.

Later that night, after the wedding, while he was chomping on a big cigar, one of the DJs came up to him, pulled out a cigarette, and called him his "tobacco friend."

They returned to London the night before he was due to start his new job. It was a Sunday evening in late summer. As expected, there was a knock at his door.

A man in a suit asked if he was Mr. _____.

He said that he was.

"Here are your keys," the man said.

Outside was a blue Saab convertible with tan leather seats. The car was fully insured, with a full tank of gas.

The next morning he got up early, climbed into the Saab, and drove.

The air was still warm outside, so he put the top down. He sped along main roads, but no highways, out of London and through Surrey, against the traffic. Just as he'd imagined, almost all the cars were going the other way—and backed up for miles—but for him it was smooth sailing.

He cruised past the open security gate and into the historic site in its valley filled with trees. He pulled into the lot of the beautiful building just off from the road.

Inside, there were two receptionists, both of whom were smoking. He checked in at the security desk and explained to the guard who he was. The guard issued him a visitor's pass and told him to sit and wait; someone would be along to welcome him.

The centrepiece in the lobby was a large replica of a Formula One racing car. It was decorated with the company's branding, and it was spectacular. The car sparkled. He sat down on a couch and marvelled at it; it made him feel like a boy.

On a nearby table were free cigarettes and newspapers for guests. He helped himself to both. People were walking in and out of the lobby, and many of them were smoking, so he lit up. He was twenty-six years old, and he felt like someone had just let him on board a pirate ship.

THE SURGEON GENERAL'S WARNING

People who haven't smoked cannot possibly understand the personal satisfaction derived from smoking a cigarette.

For many smokers, it is tantamount to having an orgasm: the exhilaration of unwrapping a vacuum-sealed package of cigarettes, popping the foil, patting the pack against your arm, and then smelling the fresh tobacco. You take the filter of the unlit cigarette and roll it around your lips. Strike the match, light the cigarette, inhale, and get that first taste of the tobacco, the flavours, and the additives.

The rush of the nicotine into the bloodstream, which numbs your senses, is unmatched by any other legal barbiturate or narcotic available on the market in the Western world. It's the feeling of the tar moving down the back of the throat, burning the esophagus, of holding the smoke in for a few seconds and then blowing it out through your nose or mouth. You can't possibly explain the pleasure achieved from this repetitive exercise. We're talking about the real smokers here. They know. The joy derived by smokers is unparalleled. Alcohol doesn't come close.

This seemingly simple device elegantly delivers a drug by the simple act of breathing in, and is perfectly designed to addict its taker. You smoke one cigarette, and then, almost mysteriously, you want another, and another. Anyone who has ever become a smoker knows this feeling of longing, and of receiving the pleasure of giving in to that longing.

Once you start, every cigarette is satisfying. And thanks to the Industrial Revolution and mechanized production, every cigarette promises precisely the same experience. A specified amount of nicotine is delivered to your brain, releasing dopamine, and in that moment you are satisfied—with morning coffee, at your lunch break, after a difficult discussion, after dinner, after drinks, after sex, in a stolen moment before you fall asleep. For a smoker, there is no end to the desire to smoke.

The lawyer just wished smoking wasn't so bad for him, and for everyone who smoked.

He'd always found it intriguing that there were no instructions on a package of cigarettes. Most consumer products had instructions, but on this special product there was nothing to indicate how it should be used. If aliens were to find a pack of cigarettes, they would have no idea what they were for. Were you supposed to eat them? Who would think to light the sticks on fire? We only learned from watching others.

He remembered watching his mother smoke. He was fascinated by her cigarette packages, which were always French—Gitanes or Gauloises. The colours and the designs of those stylish brands drew his eyes. She gave it up; he's not sure when. His father was a smoker too—pipe and cigars—and had a gentleman's smoking room, complete with brandy snifter and family photos. He read the *Globe and*

Mail cover to cover every morning, along with the *New York Times* on Sundays; the *Economist, New York Review of Books*, and *Newsweek* were scattered around the house. The lawyer couldn't recall ever having a conversation with his parents about the dangers of smoking, but he was sure that, like any parents, they would have preferred it if he didn't smoke.

He started at age fifteen and had never been interested in pot or any other drug, just cigarettes.

One day, on the subway ride home from his Toronto high school, he stopped at a convenience vendor in the station. Yes, he had a baby face, but he straightened his back and delivered his request in his most confident, deep voice: "A pack of Vantage."

Why Vantage? There was an ad for Vantage on the countertop, and he was seduced by the design: an elegant blue and red target symbol—bull's eye.

The man behind the counter looked him over, then reached behind the shelf, plucked a pack of Vantage, and slid it over. The vendor then asked the young customer for double the amount of money the pack cost. He paid, of course.

Later, he went out back to his parents' garage and unwrapped the plastic film, put the white stick in his mouth, and lit a match. He breathed in, coughed, and breathed out the smoke. It didn't feel good, but he breathed in again. It felt easier the second time.

In the movies of his teenage years—*Stand by Me, St. Elmo's Fire, The Breakfast Club, The Lost Boys*—everybody was young, vibrating with anxiety, pacing around with a cigarette as they loathed their adolescent selves. And on television there was *Miami Vice*, Don Johnson as the brooding detective leaning on his Ferrari with a cigarette, the black luminescent skin of the ocean at night reflecting the lights of the big, bad city he was patrolling; he was the good guy who loved to light a smoke after taking down a drug dealer.

It was at Boy Scout camp where the lawyer first learned to smoke socially, on weekends, and around campfires, the big flames in the middle and the little red glows of kids taking drags as they told stories, stirring the embers with branches. At home, his idol, whom he watched nightly on TV all through high school, was American talk show legend Johnny Carson. What a wonderful person Johnny was: curious, friendly, sensitive, funny, a sharp dresser, and he loved to smoke.

"I knew a man who gave up smoking, drinking, sex, and rich food. He was healthy right up until the day he killed himself," said Johnny.

The lawyer hadn't become a pack-a-day smoker until he went to university in the UK; that's when he started waking up and having a cigarette first thing. In Europe and the UK in the 1990s, he could smoke everywhere: trains, movie theatres, bars, restaurants. It was a smoker's paradise. In his residence at university, he could buy a pack from a vending machine and light up in the hallway on the way back to his room. He became a champion smoker, and he loved it.

It felt right. He was young and strong, and he could breathe easily.

Of course, he was aware of the harmful effects of smoking, but he was living in an environment where people didn't talk about that. No one seemed to care. And he wasn't experiencing any evidence of those harmful effects.

Up until the mid-1960s, tobacco companies spent hundreds of millions of dollars a year advertising their brands without criticism, and through all available channels: television, newspapers, magazines, radio, billboards, and, of course, sponsoring supersized sporting and cultural events. It was the golden age of smoking. Think *Mad Men*. Obscene amounts of money flowed and rooms were cloudy blue.

In the 1940s and '50s, it wasn't uncommon for doctors to smoke during patient consultations; it also wasn't uncommon for doctors to prescribe cigarettes as remedies for various ailments—to soothe anxiety, promote weight loss, and help with depression. Smoking was portrayed in the media as being glamorous, with health benefits, and as a surefire way to get you laid.

But in the late 1940s, before almost anyone else in the world, a doctor named Richard Doll gathered strong scientific evidence proving that smoking was a gamble, and one in which a person could lose his or her life.

Richard Doll was born in Hampton, in Greater London, in 1912, and served as an officer in World War II even as he trained in medicine. He enjoyed smoking cigarettes, and did so about five times a day. After the war, he returned to London and attended King's College, where he continued to pursue a career in medical research. He went on to become one of the world's leading epidemiologists.

By 1949, Doll was working with the Medical Research Council alongside Austin Bradford Hill, a fellow epidemiologist in London. The two researchers were trying to figure out why lung cancer rates in Britain had spiked in the first half of the twentieth century. They were intent on finding the source of the carcinogens that were invading human bodies all around them. It was old-fashioned detective work.

At first, the two doctor-detectives thought it might be because of the type of tar being used to expand Britain's road system, or other synthetic environmental pollutants popular during the postwar boom. Their method was simple and direct: they approached lung cancer patients in London hospitals and asked them to take part in a survey. The patients who agreed were asked about their family histories, diets, employment, and previous diseases they'd incurred. It turned out that of the 649 patients who had contracted lung cancer, only two were non-smokers.

Doll promptly gave up smoking his five cigarettes a day and was spurred on to find out more about the potentially deadly link between tobacco and lung cancer.

In 1951, Doll and Hill released their first report, in which they posited the relationship between smoking cigarettes and lung cancer. The report wasn't a hit among their peers; no one really wanted to hear the bad news. After all, a lot of people—including in the medical community—loved smoking. Doctors and researchers didn't want to entertain the idea that lighting up their favourite consumer brands may, in fact, be dimming once bright futures.

Doll and Hill regrouped and pushed forward. This time, instead of targeting lung cancer patients, they chose a different group to survey: doctors who smoked.

They wrote to almost sixty thousand British doctors—and we're not talking about email here; these were individual letters sent through the Royal Mail—asking them about their smoking habits and issues related to their health. It was an ingenious plan. Doll's strategy: if you, the medical community, don't trust our previous findings, here's the data gathered from the very doctors who safeguard our nation's health.

Over forty thousand doctors wrote back agreeing to take part in their smoking study. Doll and Hill published their new peer-reviewed research results in a 1954 issue of the *British Medical Journal*.

The report was groundbreaking.

Just as their earlier research had indicated, the new report firmly established the link between smoking cigarettes and lung cancer. It was remarkable, undeniable, and this time had an impact: medical researchers, scientists, and government agencies took note, on both sides of the Atlantic. Indeed, the report revealed a truth that many country doctors were already aware of—many of those rural-based medics already had a nickname for cigarettes: coffin nails.

It was Doll and Hill, though, who had established the strongest scientific link so far between tobacco use and lung cancer, and their work cleared the way, ten years later, for the US surgeon general to unleash the scientific might of America's government apparatus on its citizens.

Everything changed in 1964.

That's when the surgeon general released his landmark report containing US-based major scientific research: for the first time, the top doctor in America, along with an influential cohort of health scientists and medical researchers, categorically linked tobacco consumption to a variety of serious illnesses, cancer included.

Most people didn't know the name of the man who published that report: Luther Terry, the ninth surgeon general, who served in that position from 1961 to 1965. Yet it was Terry's report that explained what everyone now takes for granted: that smoking can kill you, and that, specifically, there is a direct link between smoking and lung cancer.

Terry's report made an impact, and the ripples it produced eventually built into a massive wave of anti-smoking sentiment that swept through mainstream society. Starting in 1969, all cigarette packs in the US had to bear the line "Warning: The Surgeon General Has Determined That Cigarette Smoking Is Dangerous to Your Health."

Most people believed that the most popular published text in the world is the Bible or the Qur'an. In fact, the surgeon general's 1964 report probably became the most often quoted publication in the history of the printed word. Phrases from it were printed in the form of warnings on billions of packs of cigarettes manufactured and sold each year, in every language, in almost every country in the world.

As the lawyer grew up, started smoking, went to university and then law school, that anti-smoking wave gathered strength.

Of course, anti-smoking campaigns had come and gone over the centuries—well before Dr. Doll's research or the US surgeon general's report. They weren't always related to physical health, and some of the early versions included sanctions far more brutal than a fine or a warning from the country's top doctor.

Just over four hundred years ago, the tobacco habit was spreading like wildfire across the populations of the world. Within decades of tobacco being imported from South America to Europe by colonial explorers, some of the most powerful rulers of that era were attempting to stamp out its use before it could take hold. Imagine reigning over a kingdom or city-state and touring the streets only to witness grey mist pouring out of your citizens' mouths and noses—eerie.

Religious leaders tried to stop it, including popes Urban VII and Innocent X, who imposed tobacco bans on clergy: neither pontiff wanted Old World church habits connected to traditions from Indigenous Nations in the New World, which utilized tobacco to communicate with the spiritual realm. Amen. We know how those early Catholic anti-smoking campaigns went: Have you ever travelled to Italy?

For a while, in the 1600s, in the Ottoman Empire and in Russia, the punishment for taking a drag became death; today, Turkey and Russia boast some of the highest smoking rates in the world. In the Eastern Himalayas, the tiny nation of Bhutan passed an anti-tobacco law as early as 1729.

Most early approaches to smoking prevention were short-lived. The addiction was simply too formidable and the experience too pleasurable.

There didn't seem to be a single leader, no matter how powerful, or a known punishment, no matter how brutal, that could stop the fire from spreading. Tobacco entered the cultures—and lungs—of every region across the planet: the global village was smoking.

In England, when King James realized he couldn't stop tobacco from spreading, His Highness decided to tax it instead, and to create a royal monopoly around the sale of this new product: taxation of tobacco became a strategy for many rulers and governments in the years ahead.

It wasn't until centuries later, in the 1930s, that scientists first began to make substantial progress linking smoking to cancer and heart disease. Among them were scientists in Germany, where health information became entwined with Nazi propaganda and warmongering. Adolf Hitler declared the smoking of tobacco to be a depraved and harmful addiction. As his armies spread across the globe, the führer waged a personal war on tobacco, instituting new taxes and bans on smoking. When the Nazis were defeated, the Reich's anti-smoking campaign was as well, and by the 1950s smoking rates were surging in both East and West Germany.

Every single anti-smoking campaign ultimately failed, and it seemed there was no way to eradicate a populace's addition to nicotine.

The 1964 US surgeon general's report seemed to be different.

It took more than three decades for those ripples from Luther Terry's report to gather into the mighty wave that crashed into the US tobacco industry in 1998. That was the year that an epic legal settlement—called the Master Settlement Agreement—was negotiated between the four largest tobacco companies in the US and the attorneys general of forty-six states.

Michael Mann's movie *The Insider* chronicles some of the dramatic backstory. It involves a tobacco executive named Jeffrey Wigand, who served as head of research and development for Brown & Williamson Tobacco, and who became famous as a whistleblower on an episode of CBS's flagship investigative news program *60 Minutes*.

Wigand claimed on 60 *Minutes* that Big Tobacco knew about the harmful effects of smoking long before Terry's report in 1964, and that it knew nicotine was addictive and had been manipulating levels of the drug in its products. The 60 *Minutes* episode featuring Wigand aired in 1995, and three years later, to avoid decades of lawsuits worth billions of dollars from dozens of US states seeking to recover tobacco-related health care costs that could have crippled the entire industry, Big Tobacco agreed to a deal: the industry would pay annual amounts in perpetuity, and a lot of them—a minimum of $206 billion over the first twenty-five years.

That's a number that would destroy almost any industry in the world, and more than a few nations, were it suddenly collected. Why would a major American industry agree to what seemed like such a raw deal? After all, their product was 100 percent legal, and quite popular.

Let's talk automobiles for a moment. While in law school, the lawyer had studied the concept of punitive damages in relation to major lawsuits levelled at big industries. In the US, the most infamous example was a case brought against one of the largest car manufacturers in the world: Ford.

In the 1970s, Ford Motor Company created the Ford Pinto, intended as a car for the masses. The Pinto made it all the way to the assembly line. Cars were ready to be shipped when, in Ford's internal testing phase, it became clear that under certain circumstances, where the car was involved in a side-impact collision, a design flaw in the fuel line could cause the Pinto to catch fire.

Instead of recalling the cars and fixing the problem, the court hearing the case was told, Ford had pursued a different business strategy. Ford calculated the likely damages the company would have to pay to customers and their families as the result of collision accidents versus the cost of a recall and full redesign. It concluded that it would be cheaper to pay the claims and continue with the status quo rather than pull the plug and start again. An internal Ford document with grim calculations was paraded in front of the court and its jury. Not surprisingly, as Pintos were sold, people started being injured, and some were dying in fiery explosions.

In this particular case, *Grimshaw v. Ford Motor Company*, the court awarded the plaintiff, Richard Grimshaw, punitive damages of $120 million. That was a surprise. No one expected a number that big.

The concept of punitive damages is as it implies: the legal system imposes punishment beyond the normal tariff damages equal to the loss that had been suffered. The Pinto case created a new fear for corporations. Courts could punish a company for acting badly, basically, and the Pinto case proved that they would. If financial pain changed behaviour, the larger the company, the higher the punitive damages had to be.

Ford, let's keep in mind, was a very large company, but not as large as all four major American tobacco companies combined. Hence, a question began to pop up in legal circles in the aftermath of the Pinto verdict: What would happen if those large tobacco companies were ever faced with punitive damages in a US court of law?

No one knew the answer to that multi-billion-dollar question — or was it a trillion-dollar question?

Another consideration: the tobacco lobby had tremendous power in Washington.

Cigarette smoking was big business in terms of manufacturing, production, and marketing, as well as sales and distribution. It was a healthy American agricultural crop, a lucrative source of tax revenue, and a product enjoyed by tens of millions of loyal customers, if not more.

It went deeper, though. The industry had been a cornerstone of the fledgling United States economy, with some estimates suggesting that tobacco excise taxes accounted for as much as one-third of the young nation's tax revenue—just one reason perhaps that the emblem of tobacco leaves was embedded atop some of the Corinthian columns supporting the US Capitol buildings.

By the 1990s, the mounting threat of litigation against the tobacco industry was starting to cause internal concern to the industry. Despite the fact that many headline-grabbing damages were awarded in the US, they were often overturned on appeal. In the Pinto case, that initial award of $120 million was reduced dramatically, to $2 million (perhaps a lot of money for a citizen to receive, but not for a large company to pay out).

The US was an interesting legal jurisdiction in that it had trial by jury for civil matters. So here's a scenario: you took a sick person suffering from emphysema—or any other of the 250 illnesses known to be related to tobacco use—and stuck that individual in a courtroom in view of a jury. That person was hooked up to a respirator and seated across the floor from a bunch of tobacco executives in expensive suits. You pulled the heartstrings of the jury by making the case that, but for the horrific products this industry manufactured, this sick person—a God-fearing and hard-working American —would be healthy and happy.

How do you think the jury would rule?

Some lawyers imagined that if they could show the tobacco companies had been negligent, they could win a fortune larger than the GDP of some nations. It was an Erin Brockovich moment waiting to happen.

Punitive Damages +
Surgeon General's Warning +
Wave of Anti-Smoking Attitudes =
$$ from tobacco companies

Let's add another X factor to the equation: no one actually knew what caused cancer.

Smoking caused cancer in some smokers, yes. But the medical community still hadn't learned why some smokers but not all smokers developed cancer. It remains a scientific mystery—one for our children to solve in the better future we all dream of.

Everybody, though, was now aware of the risks associated with smoking. You'd have to be an ostrich living in North Korea to get around the failure to warn clause. The term *failure to warn* was self-explanatory: there wasn't a living adult soul in this world who did not know that smoking caused cancer, that it was bad for you, and that it could kill you. That was thanks to Luther Terry's report and to those warnings printed on billions of packs of cigarettes.

In the meantime, apparently, an incredible payday awaited some ambitious law firm, but no one could prove the case and get around this complex scenario of obstacles in terms of a lawsuit.

Then Jeffrey Wigand entered the public arena in the mid-1990s, just as the lawyer was entering law school and becoming a committed chain-smoker.

As a former head of research and development for Big Tobacco, Wigand said that the tobacco companies knew their product was addictive and that it would kill you, and they didn't tell the public. And Wigand had proof: documents and experience.

Now it was a different ballgame. Now it wasn't about failure to warn; it was about failure to put forward all the evidence the manufacturer was keeping to itself. This was called "withholding pertinent information."

Wigand's revelation was of particular interest to US states, that were spending fortunes covering health care costs for millions of Americans who smoked. After Wigand appeared on American prime-time TV, the threat of a new round of litigation became very real, and in the background, dozens of states were working together, organizing a strategy to go after tobacco companies in pack formation. The industry was put on its back foot, and there was a cliff behind it, below which lay financial oblivion.

Let's throw in one more X factor: the political pressure bearing down on the US federal government.

The Clinton administration was in power, and the president and his advisers worried about the looming showdown between Big Tobacco and the US states. The administration didn't want to be in charge while a major historic industry was burned to the ground.

The Clinton administration wanted to regulate the industry but didn't know how to do it. It wanted to tax the product more heavily than ever, too, as many countries were doing, but this was America and people didn't like taxes. And to protect children and minors, it wanted to restrict the companies' marketing capabilities, but it was mindful of the Constitution and its guaranteed freedom of speech. The administration concluded it couldn't tax consumers further, and it couldn't pass new laws restricting freedom of speech.

But what could it do?

To explore a Hail Mary possibility, the government entered into a complex dialogue with the industry that stretched over two years, and here was the final offer: in exchange for protection from all US states intent on suing Big Tobacco, the industry would agree to make a very large payout, as well as agree to voluntary concessions around the sale of most of its products and much of its advertising.

In the wake of Wigand and the hunt by the attorneys general, the tobacco industry didn't have a lot of options. So it agreed to dismantle its lobby in Washington; it agreed to impose marketing and advertising restrictions on its products; and it agreed to increase consumer awareness programs that explained the dangers of smoking—for example, the nonprofit Truth Initiative, which was based in Washington and dedicated to educating youth on the dangers of smoking. In addition, the industry would restrict access to tobacco products.

A manufacturer restricting consumer access to its product—that was rare in America.

Perhaps most importantly, the industry agreed to a payment of $206 billion over the first twenty-five years.

Two hundred billion dollars and change.

Perspective: El Chapo, the Mexican drug lord/entrepreneur, claimed in 2016 that his fortune was estimated by *Forbes* at one billion dollars. Those are profits from a lifetime of work by one of the most successful drug dealers in the world. Let's assume that number isn't accurate, since we're talking about a drug dealer's empire.

More respectable: Apple Inc. was estimated to have amassed— after creating the iMac, the MacBook, the iPod, the iPad, iTunes, and the iPhone, among other groundbreaking products—a fortune of about $200 billion over its first forty years.

An interstellar comparison: it has been surmised that the sun in our sky is one of about two hundred billion stars in the Milky Way galaxy.

This massive amount of money would be demanded from tobacco companies and used to fund state health care and anti-tobacco programs. All big tobacco companies were "encouraged" to participate, and all the major companies did.

Indeed, they really had no choice.

Here's what the industry gained from the deal: protection.

All pending lawsuits from all US states immediately went away, with no possibility of future lawsuits. It was an expensive legal miracle.

The price of the product went up, but the Master Settlement Agreement payments (those billions of dollars) were passed on to the consumer and not to the tobacco companies. It was Jill and Joe Smoker who were actually footing the massive bill, and over a long period of time. The extra charge on each pack wasn't considered a tax. This was a brilliant, made-in-America solution.

Of course, the entire industry had to dismantle its lobby groups in Washington. So goodbye political influence and backroom brokering in private, smoky dining lounges. Those days were over.

Most importantly, from the lawyer's perspective, the marketing and advertising restrictions for cigarettes completely changed.

The industry agreed to stop any form of tobacco advertising that could be perceived as appealing to minors. The cartoonish Joe Camel had to go; the Marlboro Man had to ride off into the sunset; billboard advertising had to cease. But here was the good news: these new restrictions applied to every major tobacco company, so no individual company had to worry about an unfair advantage given to its competitor.

The lawyer started his job in the tobacco industry in the late summer of 2001, just three years after the Master Settlement Agreement was signed in the US, and as waves from the surgeon general's report continued to roll outward—changing social attitudes and laws in almost every nation on Earth—they gathered in strength and were finally crashing on the shores of Spain, France, Italy, Greece, and the United Kingdom.

The lawyer's new job was to help the company navigate those fast-moving legal waters, making sure its marketing and ad campaigns were complying in full with the new laws and restrictions descending on the UK marketplace—all while selling as many cigarettes as possible.

It was an exciting time to be joining the industry. No other consumer product was quite like cigarettes. The fact that cigarettes were still 100 percent legal while at the same time proven to be deadly had created a kind of paradox which swirled mysteriously at the centre of this special product's popularity.

As far as the lawyer could tell, given everything he knew about smoking, cigarettes shouldn't even have been available as a mass market product. Capitalism, it seemed, hadn't been designed to contain this particular consumer anomaly.

It had been decades since Richard Doll, and then the surgeon general, had found cigarettes to be poisonous. Yet here he was, a young lawyer, joining a corporate multinational company which manufactured and sold this product around the globe. Even more absurd, he was a smoker. He was sailing full speed into the tobacco paradox, not sure what to expect.

NORTHERN IRISH FACTORY

On his first day of work at the new company, the lawyer was promptly greeted at reception by a bubbly personal assistant, who led him to the elevator banks.

They rode to the top floor of the building, which housed the board of directors and the legal department. She walked him into the heart of legal and introduced him to the other personal assistants, including his own, Nancy.

"What kind of cigarettes do you smoke?" Nancy asked.

Nancy was about sixty-five, convivial, and had some edge: she wore a short skirt, stylish boots, and a tight low-cut top. She showed him to the office he'd already seen, with its large desk and spectacular view of the grounds and the forest.

He didn't smoke any of their brands. Since living in England, he'd switched from Vantage, which was almost impossible to find, to Peter Stuyvesant. But he told her the name of a cigarette they manufactured.

"I'll make sure your cigarette tray is filled with them every evening," she offered graciously.

Nancy gave him a comprehensive tour of the compound.

They revisited the restaurant, which served a full sit-down lunch every day; they visited the medical office, staffed by a resident nurse. He was required to have a full medical examination in his first month at the company, including a chest X-ray. When he did, the X-ray came back clear. Thank god. He'd never heard of a company that screened their employees for cancer.

Back in the lawyer's spacious new office, Nancy showed him an agenda that had been prepared for his first few weeks with the company. He scanned the document, and it became clear he wouldn't be doing legal work anytime soon; instead, it was as if he were going back to school.

Then Mary came in and greeted him warmly.

Mary was his supervisor; her supervisor was the legal team's captain, a.k.a. general counsel, and the general reported to the CEO.

Mary added context to his agenda. It was important for him to understand this business, she explained, in order to defend it. He needed to be educated on how tobacco products were made, how they were marketed, and how they were sold. His early days would be a series of study sessions and informational seminars focused on these areas — as well as a few field trips. This process for management employees who were learning about the inner workings of their new company was called "inductions."

He'd be absorbing a lot of knowledge about the basics of tobacco over his first month.

One of the first steps in his education was touring the company's factory in Northern Ireland.

It was located about an hour outside of Belfast, and the region was an important one for the company. In 1896, as business rapidly expanded, they'd built what was then the largest cigarette factory in the world.

Now, just over one hundred years later, the lawyer was on his way to visit the company's last cigarette factory in the UK. As more and more people cut down on smoking or stopped altogether, factories were being shuttered: the one in Hyde, Manchester; the one in Northolt, London. History.

The factory in Northern Ireland was still humming, though, and keeping it open allowed the company to print five very important words on every pack: "Made in the United Kingdom," a must-have feature for customer loyalty.

Believe it or not, in the global village, people still cared about buying things that were manufactured in their own country and made by their fellow citizens. National pride wasn't dead yet—as Brexit later went on to prove.

Several things struck the lawyer the first time he travelled for the company.

One: the whole trip was organized for him by Nancy—his tickets, itinerary, hotel room, agenda, everything. He just had to show up and go along for the ride. Sit and listen, kid.

Two: a driver picked him up for his journey to the airport.

Three: he flew in business class.

He'd never been to Belfast before, and he was a little nervous.

The Troubles in Northern Ireland had officially ended in 1998, but the uneasy spirit of those times still felt very much alive in early 2001, and before he left, his fiancée told him she was concerned. He waved it off as no big deal. And it really wasn't, because he was travelling inside the corporate bubble: he needed only to step into the limo, arrive at the business-class lounge, jet over, take the car awaiting him with driver, cruise to the factory, return to the hotel, drive back to the airport, jet home. There was very little chance of encountering anything that might be a threat—or authentic.

The flight from Heathrow was fast—less than an hour—and he was served a hot breakfast. He noticed other company employees in business class whom he had seen at HQ but not yet met. This was clearly a route that was well travelled by the company.

The view from the airplane window as he flew into Ireland at dawn was mesmerizing: the rocky shoreline and blue of the sea; the white froth of the crashing waves; the rolling fields over low hills; the shifting greens of those pastures.

He was greeted at Belfast International Airport by his driver, Madeleine. Friendly and professional, she informed him that their journey to the factory would take about forty-five minutes. She drove; she did not smoke.

The scenery on the ground was not as beautiful as it had been from above. They passed sectarian imagery, graffiti, paving stones painted with Union Jacks, IRA scrawl, slogans in support of the UUP and Sinn Féin. For thirty years this had been a sort of war zone, and some of those battle scars remained etched on the urban landscape.

He watched it all pass him by from the back of the town car, where to his delight he found a selection of cigarettes, bottled water, and magazines.

It was the first time he'd ever visited a cigarette factory, and he was excited—as a consumer. How many people actually toured the factories that manufactured the products they used on a daily, weekly, or monthly basis and had the chance to see how they were made?

The factory compound was gated and tightly guarded, Madeleine informed him. He noted the contract security personnel patrolling the grounds, and she pointed out government customs officers roaming around in official uniform. He thought it a bit odd, seeing a government security presence at a manufacturing plant.

"This is a bonded facility," Madeleine said.

Bonded meant that the company was able to manufacture and warehouse taxable goods on the premises and had paid the duty on those goods, which was why the place was under the UK government's watchful and protective eye.

Essentially, the company made the goods here, cut a cheque to the government for each and every pack, and then the goods were stored on-site in the equivalent of a government-guarded vault, and eventually citizens would also pay a tax at the point of sale, usually the convenience store counter.

When the car came to a stop, a man was waiting for him: Conor, an executive with the company.

Conor greeted him with a sharp Ulster accent. The lawyer could only understand what Conor was saying when Conor Spoke. Very. Slowly.

Off they went into the factory's executive offices, where Conor offered him a cup of tea. Compared to the headquarters in London, the place was extremely rundown. The space didn't look as if it had been renovated for forty years, and there were old ashtrays and the smell of stale cigarettes everywhere.

He looked out the window and saw an old fountain feature in the courtyard that he guessed hadn't worked since the 1970s. The place was kind of depressing. Of course, it didn't need to feel cheerful, because none of this part of the company was public-facing. They were behind the manufacturing curtain.

Conor explained what was on the agenda for the next couple of days. (Everyone, it seemed, had their own company agenda, prepared by their own personal assistant.) Conor's agenda was to show the lawyer around the factory so he could see first-hand how cigarettes were manufactured and then take him to meet the research and development executives, who would explain the contemporary issues related to creating a cigarette. The factory doubled as the headquarters of the company's R & D division.

Though the lawyer had smoked for years, he knew almost nothing about the manufacturing process of cigarettes, and ditto about R & D. Conor was taking him through a version of Tobacco University.

The lawyer told Conor a little bit about how he'd arrived at the company. As they chatted in Conor's office, the lawyer reached into his pocket and pulled out his pack of cigarettes.

Conor stopped and looked at him.

"Where did you get those?" he asked.

"I brought them in with me."

Conor laughed. "You can't be found in here smoking those. If a customs guard stops you, you have no proof that you bought them in a store. You could have stolen them off the line."

Conor opened a cupboard and showed the lawyer. It was crammed with packs identical to the one the lawyer was smoking, but for one important distinction: a special small ink stamp on each package indicated it was allowed to be smoked within the factory.

"These are for use inside the premises. It shows we've paid the tax on these. Any time you come here in the future, just ask me for cigarettes," Conor said. He handed the lawyer a fresh ink-stamped pack of smokes and protective gear to wear: a white coat, a helmet, and a pair of goggles.

The lawyer felt like a construction-site inspector as he adjusted his goggles and followed Conor onto the factory floor.

Conor explained that there were four areas to this facility: receiving, processing, packaging, and the bonded government area where the finished product was counted and guarded before it was shipped out to destinations across Europe and beyond.

Conor showed the lawyer the massive receiving area first. This was where the "leaf" came in.

"Leaf is raw tobacco," Conor explained.

It arrived in large bales—each about the size of a household dishwasher—from all over the world: Turkey, regions of Africa, the

US, and the lawyer's birth country, Canada. The company had a dedicated leaf-hunting department with a mission to search the planet to secure a constant, high-quality, low-cost supply of Virginia leaf for factories like this one.

Virginia was the *crème de la crème* of tobacco leaf, according to Conor.

British tobacco products were mostly made from Virginia leaf: Dunhill, Benson & Hedges, and so on. Then there was burley (American) leaf: think Marlboro, Lucky Strike, Winston. American leaf had a totally different taste.

Virginia leaf went all the way back to the founding of the English colony of Virginia and beyond.

When the British first settled in Virginia and experimented with different agricultural yields to ship back to Europe, tobacco was seen to be particularly valuable, because demand for it at home was climbing off the charts.

But tobacco wasn't easy to farm and conditions were harsh. Colonial settlers just couldn't seem to stay alive very long while harvesting the New World weed. So even as the British invested in tobacco farming, sending boatloads of new settler blood to do so, that blood drained fast. This challenge was partially alleviated when a Dutch ship sailed into harbour transporting a cargo of enslaved Africans. Their forced labour proved vital for providing a steady supply of Virginia leaf to satisfy Britain's fast-evolving love affair with nicotine—and it resulted in the establishment of the American tobacco industry.

Now, the company had leaf representatives who scoured the world, exploring far-flung locations and keeping close track of where Virginia leaf was being grown, and by whom, and buying it up at auctions. This Northern Irish factory was where that leaf was sent for processing. Bales of tobacco leaf didn't cost a lot of money—tobacco companies had for over a century devised strategies to keep those prices low at the expense of farmers—but they did take up a lot of room.

"Clean it, dry it, toast it, blend it," Conor said, and then repeated the phrase, as if it were his mantra. "Clean it, dry it, toast it, blend it."

The first step was to wash those giant bales of leaf.

They paused to watch a man whose job it was to load the raw bundles of leaf into supersized storage containers by driving a forklift back and forth over a very short distance, piling giant bundles up into his lift and dumping them into the mouth of the ever-hungry containers, which led to the washing units. The man knew when he had to refill a container based on a single light that blinked on and off.

Reload the forklift, wait for that light to blink on. Repeat.

This micro-journey was the guy's entire day, every day, every week. The lawyer had never seen an industrialized process like this up close before.

The massive containers fed the leaf into the biggest washing machines you could possibly imagine; each washing machine was as big as your entire basement. What came out was damp tobacco mulch—massive heaps of primordial brown mush.

The smell of tobacco was very strong, and it was not at all like the stench of stale smoke and dirty ashtrays back in the factory offices. This was sweet fresh tobacco being dried and toasted, and its scent was delicious. The lawyer couldn't get enough of it.

They strolled deeper into the factory. It was huge, the size of an indoor football field, and filled with machinery.

For a highly automated process, though, a lot of people were involved. Hundreds of workers along the lines made sure their piece of the operation was running smoothly. Conveyor belts lead off every which way. He'd never really watched conveyor belts before, and he wasn't the only one watching them. It was basically what these employees did all day: monitoring, taking things off the lines, trouble-shooting. They all wore matching green work pants and shirts.

Not a single employee on the lines spoke to the lawyer or Conor as they strolled by. They weren't being distant or rude; it was just that no one needed to communicate with them. It was also incredibly loud. The lawyer listened to the constant hum and felt the massive shaking and stirring of all those machines.

"This is a loyal workforce," Conor explained.

Many workers were the third or fourth generation of a family who had worked for this factory, he said. The family relationship could stretch all the way back to the era of the company founder, who had started selling handmade cigarettes in Belfast at the turn of the twentieth century.

In the late 1800s, cigarettes were hand-rolled and sold straight off a cart or out of a shack.

The fastest cigarette rollers could spin about four cigarettes a minute. Have you ever rolled a cigarette? Try rolling four in sixty seconds. It's a rare skill set.

Legend had it that the company's founder started out rolling cigarettes solo and selling them off a cart in Ireland (before the country was partitioned), and he gained a loyal customer base. He did so well, he made the journey to London and opened a shop in the City (not too far from where the lawyer first met with Heather, the headhunter).

In London, the Irish tobacco entrepreneur's hand-rolled cigarettes continued to attract devout customers. He hired more rollers.

Soon, packaging evolved: cigarettes were being tied together in bundles, sometimes with decorative paper wrapping, and then with a cardboard insert, which stabilized the bundle—the first cigarette packs, basically. That stabilizer card also offered the first real chance to add signature branding. It became known as a cigarette card, and artful early versions of those cards later became valuable to collectors.

As the market for hand-rolled cigarettes surged—surpassing chewing tobacco, cigars, and snuff—one leading American cigarette manufacturer offered a $75,000 reward to any innovator who could build a machine that would speed up the process and roll cigarettes mechanically. By this time, after all, the Industrial Revolution had transformed the world, and many consumer goods were already being manufactured by machine.

A young entrepreneurial dreamer called James Bonsack answered the call. He created a machine that could roll about two hundred cigarettes a minute, or more than one hundred thousand a day. The machine could do this by rolling one very long, giant cigarette, which was then sliced into smaller, normal-sized lengths.

Cigarettes could have remained an artisanal, handmade indulgence, but Bonsack's machine was a game-changer, circa 1880.

Suddenly, the Bonsack machine and its imitators meant that cigarette companies could fire their hand-rollers and redirect profits towards a new trend: advertising campaigns. Many companies did so, and business boomed. Cigarettes had become cheap to make and cheap to buy—and were addictive.

Powerful tobacco empires emerged in Britain and America, including the company which the lawyer now represented, and over the early twentieth century those empires grew even stronger, aggressively expanding their customer bases and transforming cigarettes into a successful mass market consumer good. The industry's profits shot upward, just like the cities it sold to. In the shining, modern metropolis, men and women, rich or poor—and children too—smoked by the tens of millions, consuming billions of cigarettes a year. It was the perfect, industrious drug for the workforce and its overlords, delivering a constant pleasure without the effect of inebriation—so a person could smoke and work, at the same time.

Maybe smoke should have been the official colour of the early twentieth century. It rose from thousands of newly humming factories, from between the fingers of the expanding industrialized workforce, and from the lips of the industry barons, builders of unspeakable fortunes, blowing smoke rings from behind their imposing desks.

"Employees are well looked after," Conor emphasized.

These were good, stable jobs, and the company strove to be the kind of employer that took care of its people, with excellent pay, in a safe environment—unless you considered free cigarettes on the job a hazard.

Staff at the factory received complimentary cigarettes, and because they weren't allowed to take home tobacco products, it was a "smoke all you can" policy at the factory. Employees weren't allowed to smoke while working on the lines, but there were break areas for them. The lawyer thought of Nancy offering to fill his tray with cigarettes each morning at HQ.

Still, Conor said, any employee who had worked here for years was aware that fewer staff were visible on the floor—and not just because technology was improving.

As the number of smokers declined in the twenty-first century, there was less need for tobacco manufacturing. The lawyer commented that not all the manufacturing lines were in use, and Conor nodded. The Irishman gestured to some old cigar lines that were closed that day. These lines were simply empty, the big machines silent.

After the tobacco was washed, it was dried and toasted and then blended into specific brands—just like mixing different cocktails. The company had more than twenty-five brands of cigarettes on the market.

Flavourings, additives, and chemicals were mixed with the leaf according to the specific recipe for that particular brand. Broadly speaking, most traditional English brands didn't have a lot of flavourings; Virginia tobacco was considered a beautiful cured leaf and you didn't want to mess with it too much. It would be like ordering a triple-A Alberta beef filet mignon and dumping HP Sauce all over it.

When the raw ingredient was the finest in the world, you wanted to add only a few things: oils, some sugar, some cocoa. Every added ingredient had a purpose, and in some cases had been time-tested for decades to ensure it suited the taste of the consumer: the freshness of the product; the way the product behaved when it was lit; the way those ingredients tasted and smelled while they burned and were inhaled.

Chemicals were added to control the cigarette's burn and to achieve specific levels of tar and nicotine delivery, as well as— believe it or not—make the ash look more attractive: ash grey.

Conor took the lawyer to the mouth of a giant machine where the leaf was being blended and told him it was okay to reach in and grab a handful of tobacco. The lawyer did so and raised it up to his nose. The scent was overwhelming.

Once batches of leaf had been transformed into specific brands, those brand batches then had to be formed into cigarettes, or "sticks."

These manufacturing machines had come a long way since Bonsack's invention. They reminded the lawyer of a machine gun, the way they shot out sticks at high speed. The blended tobacco flowed into the machine, which was loaded with cork-coloured tipping paper and filters. It shot out piles of cigarettes: boom, boom, boom. These weren't the cigarettes you're used to seeing, though; they emerged as pieces twice the length of a cigarette, with the filter in the middle. A blade then sliced the filter in half, and presto: two fresh sticks.

This single factory created billions of sticks a year, according to Conor.

Next came packaging: a different machine fed twenty or twenty-five freshly cut sticks at a time into packs that anyone would recognize —world-famous brands—and then those packs were mechanically gathered into cartons and wrapped snugly in plastic.

In some cases, the packaging of cigarettes cost more than the sticks inside them. That's because each pack was lined with specialized paper encasing the sticks, tucked inside a glossy card-print case that was vacuum-sealed in plastic—the evolution of tying up bundles of hand-rolled cigarettes with a card propping the whole thing up.

But the concept was still the same, and so much of what a customer was buying came down to a recognizable brand—their dependable old friend who would never change.

The most expensive feature of a pack was certainly no longer the tobacco; it wasn't the glossy cardboard, either; and it wasn't even the expensive paper that lined each pack. It was often a little stamp printed on the pack for government customs.

In many markets, this tax stamp was called a banderole, and it represented the tobacco duty, or tax, that was imposed by the government in whose territory it was being sold. In France at the time, for example, the duty was about two euros per pack—so each French stamp was worth two euros and indicated that the pack had been cleared to move through the country's sales system by the customs department.

As Conor pointed out, billions of sticks were rolling off the lines each year at this factory; after all, the company had control of 40 percent of the UK's tobacco market alone. Packs made on the premises were being sent to destinations across Europe, Asia, Africa, and the Middle East. When the lawyer looked more closely at different cartons rolling off the line, he noticed health warnings in multiple languages: English, French, Spanish, German, and Arabic—a reminder that he worked for an international operation.

As he surveyed the multilingual health warnings, he realized that he and Conor hadn't discussed health factors on this tour. There had been nothing at all to indicate that what these workers were manufacturing was considered dangerous. It was as if they were making cola or potato chips.

Conor led him to the fourth area: the bonded, guarded facility within the factory overseen by a staff of government officers.

This area was quite possibly one of the most secure, heavily protected zones in the entire United Kingdom. Inside were walls of cigarette cartons, tens of thousands of them, millions of sticks just waiting there, ready for shipment globally.

The lawyer had never seen so many cartons of cigarettes in one place. He did some quick mental arithmetic: the store he was looking at was worth hundreds of millions of dollars. It was like standing in a vault filled with stacks of bullion.

As he looked around him, he realized that although cigarettes were mostly just dried leaves and paper, they were actually worth more than their weight in gold. There was no question every one of these tens of thousands of packs would be sold, each of them bought by a smoker like him, guaranteed.

Management at the company understood the astounding value of this product: after all, they were among the privileged few who controlled and reaped the profits from this immensely popular and addictive consumer product, selling it to the masses who were its heaviest users, including those working on the factory floor churning it out.

———

He'd always thought that the Industrial Revolution was something to learn about in history class—an era that had passed. His visit changed his perspective on that point. It was still happening.

That was the lawyer's major takeaway from his factory visit: sticks were "cheap as chips" to make, and because the Industrial Revolution was still paying dividends, the company continued to make its fortune, even as it absorbed the hits from the ongoing global anti-tobacco assault.

Every brand he saw being created on the factory floor began with its own special recipe: unique ingredients and flavourings. Those recipes were the tightly guarded secrets of research and development—and likely the most controversial combination of ingredients in the history of mainstream consumer products.

The first step in the lawyer's education was complete. The inductions, it turned out, were kind of like the lawyer's own little closed-circuit interview show, where he had a chance to chat with and personally interview key employees and teams at his new company: he didn't have a couch, a desk, or a live band, but it *was* fun, and informative.

He followed Conor to his next meeting, to visit the recipe-keepers.

PLAYING WITH FIRE

If all of those machines and thousands of employees in green uniforms on the factory floor were the brawn of the company, the white-coats in research and development formed the big, nerdy brain. It has been the purpose of R & D divisions since their inception: to function as creative brains to invent profitable new products for the company.

Way back in the late 1870s—as the company was expanding its cigarette business in the UK—Thomas Edison set up a research lab across the Atlantic, in upstate New York, where he and his team invented what we now take for granted: the electric light bulb.

Edison had many bright ideas, and one was to recruit imaginative thinkers and scientists focused on innovating new products for his fledgling Edison Electric Light Company. In other words, he was an early American adopter of a research and development department.

The concept of employing highly skilled creative minds to think outside the box for a commercial company wasn't exactly new, but it definitely wasn't the norm. Edison was an outlier and a scientific genius who was more adept at dreaming big than running a big business. Eventually, his Edison Electric Light Company was forced to merge with its major competitors to create what was becoming the trend in the New World at that time: a corporation.

The result of the merger was General Electric, and it became one of only twelve companies listed on the Dow Jones Industrial Average when the index launched in 1896—alongside other rapidly growing US ventures in cotton, oil, and rubber, and including the American Tobacco Company.

Scientists and physicists who worked with GE's R & D team went on to earn multiple Nobel Prizes, and GE's research lab evolved to be a leader in the R & D sector, changing global corporate culture. Companies across the world played catch-up, recruiting top scientists, engineers, chemists, mathematicians, astrophysicists, and brainy inventors into their nascent R & D ranks.

World War II added heat to the winning R & D formula, fusing corporate research with government agendas—as well as government funding—in the quest to create new tech to help defeat the Axis forces. The chemical company DuPont, for example, launched its version of an R & D department in 1903, calling it "an experimental station," and by the time World War II erupted, DuPont was in a strong position to contribute valuable research and resources to the Manhattan Project. The atomic bomb was a group effort.

Boom! Not only had research and development departments become mainstream, they were heroes who had helped end the war. And in the postwar era, tobacco companies followed the trend, investing heavily in R & D, at first with the hope of innovating their immensely popular consumer products, and then increasingly to defend those products against the growing ranks of leading scientists and medical practitioners who were sounding the alarm on the cigarette.

It was during the 1950s, with Doll's report, and then the 1960s, with the US surgeon general's report, that all major tobacco companies began turning down the dial on creative inventing and cranking up damage control, directing their R & D labs to examine the evidence being gathered that linked their product to the sky-rocketing rates of lung cancer. Their public responses were famously controversial: opaque science or outright denials. Fake news, it's now called.

These fiercely competitive tobacco empires even banded together to form the absurdly titled Tobacco Industry Research Committee, hiring more scientists, along with PR firms, to combat the rising health warnings in a coordinated effort to slow the effect of medical research on public opinion.

They fired an infamous volley on January 4, 1954, when a two-page advertorial in the *New York Times* promised that American tobacco companies were using cutting-edge science to safeguard their products.

> In charge of the research activities of the Committee will be a scientist of unimpeachable integrity and national repute. In addition there will be an Advisory Board of scientists disinterested in the cigarette industry. A group of distinguished men from medicine, science, and education will be invited to serve on this Board. These scientists will advise the Committee on its research activities.

The strategy worked. Using the cover of science and research to beat back public panic with obfuscation, the tobacco companies pretended they were bolstering their R & D departments with health scientists intent on exposing any hidden dangers lurking inside the product. In doing so, R & D departments at tobacco companies became inextricably linked to the defence of the product—and the promise that it was neither addictive nor harmful.

Ultimately, of course, the detailed conclusions of the medical establishment came to the forefront of public discourse, with help from the surgeon general, and those conclusions were irrefutable and grim.

Medical researchers released public lists of chemicals hidden in the curl of smoke rising from a mouth: six hundred chemicals had been found in the ingredient list for cigarettes, but the shocker really came once the stick was set on fire.

Fire changed things. It destroyed, sure, but it also created, and it turned out that more than seven thousand chemicals were released when flames consumed a cigarette.

And, wow, it was a nasty list, currently available on the American Lung Association website: acetone, found in nail polish remover; acetic acid, an ingredient in hair dye; ammonia, a common household cleaner; arsenic, used in rat poison; benzene, found in rubber cement and gasoline; butane, used in lighter fluid; cadmium, an active component in battery acid; formaldehyde, used in embalming fluid; hexamine, found in barbecue lighter fluid; lead, used in batteries; naphthalene, an ingredient in mothballs; methanol, a main component in rocket fuel; toluene, used to manufacture paint.

Butane or rocket fuel may sound terrible, but even when it came to an ingredient as seemingly benign as cocoa . . . well, when cocoa burned it transformed into a carcinogen: a cancerous cocoa puff.

And just to make matters so much worse, nicotine turned out to be ferociously addictive—up there with cocaine and heroin. The poisonous cloud entering the lungs was a shortcut to happiness, releasing dopamine, seducing the brain into wanting more of it, and then more, please. It would never be enough.

As late as 1994, that concept of nicotine dependence was still being debated. That was the year the CEOs of all major American tobacco companies testified in front of Congress—as well as CNN's cameras—that cigarettes were not addictive. That really wasn't cool, to lie to everyone under oath like that, and on television.

In light of all the evidence, Robert Proctor, Stanford historian and author of *Golden Holocaust*, described the cigarette this way: "The cigarette is the deadliest artifact in the history of human civilization."

By 2001, it was hard to imagine a more vilified group than the research and development team for a multinational tobacco company; they were up there with arms manufacturers and heroin dealers. Unlike their R & D predecessors from World War II, the product development teams at tobacco companies were reviled as supervillains.

But when Conor walked the lawyer into this den of wolves, this was what he encountered: a warm, considerate, and amazingly friendly group of people curious to meet the new counsel.

The R & D team all wore white lab coats, and he was invited by their vice-president to tour the laboratories and then sit for a cup of tea with his new company peers. There was no team on Earth, really, who knew cigarettes more intimately than the people he was meeting with now.

Every cigarette ever manufactured in this factory had started with a formula, or "recipe," created and refined here in R & D. Historically, they were the recipe-keepers at the company, and those recipes had turned out to be even more valuable than the warehouse full of cartons of cigarettes he'd just gawked at—those bars of gold.

In the era of global industrialized capitalism, an original confidential recipe for a popular consumer product had become one of the most precious commodities. Think Heinz ketchup, Coca-Cola, or Kentucky Fried Chicken. These famous brands crossed international boundaries, transcended politics and even economic class divisions. They had become a part of the global family cupboard.

And in the hyper-competitive tobacco industry, it was recipes—along with their branded identities—that set one cigarette apart from another, providing the distinct taste and smell of a particular blend when it was set alight and inhaled. For Jill and Joe Smoker, these qualities were as familiar and dependable as an Oreo cookie.

Recipes, he learned, weren't registered as intellectual property, because the life of the patent was only about twenty years. That's why Coke had never patented its Coca-Cola classic recipe, or why KFC never did so for its chicken. They're called secret recipes for a reason—and, in fact, they were trade secrets.

Some of the recipes guarded by the tobacco company, the lawyer was informed, had been created by the founder in the late 1800s and time-tested and perfected over a hundred years, passed down from one generation to the next, from one R & D team to the next.

That's why R & D's primary responsibility, above all else, was quality control. It was their mission to make sure the formula for every single stick was consistent with what the customer expected. Their job was to engineer the perfect cigarette experience, making sure it burned the way the customer wanted it to, and controlling the taste that hit the tongue just so, the density of the smoke rolling around the mouth, the amount of nicotine absorbed into the bloodstream and the brain, the rate at which carbon monoxide entered the lungs, and the way it felt when a smoker inhaled and exhaled—all the good and all the bad that was neatly rolled up in their product.

The mood in the R & D laboratory on his visit was surprisingly positive.

He suspected that the white-coats were excited to be here in the same way he was. It was challenging, engaging work: the people in R & D got to work in cutting-edge science in toxicology and epidemiology, and he would soon be grappling with complex legal issues.

The white-coats worked out of a sprawling 1960s addition to the old factory—a modernist wing with a layout designed for a bygone era when suited men had ruled over the business from the factory itself, their palatial offices each equipped with a secretary perched at a desk with a typewriter outside the executive's door.

Now, of course, the executives and assistants had moved to the London HQ, and this wing was R & D's domain.

The vice-president of R & D walked the lawyer through the sprawling space. Large windows, and fluorescents above, flooded the area with light. It glinted off the chrome detailing of the vintage office furniture and metal pedestal ashtrays that punctuated a floor of durable linoleum sweeping through the wide hallways and common areas. It all smelled of stale smoke.

Some of the grand old offices had been converted into labs that kind of felt like high school science classrooms, with Bunsen burners, microscopes, scalpels, and computer equipment. In one of those rooms, a white-coated woman was in the process of taking apart a relatively new addition to the cigarette landscape: a Marlboro Light.

This was called a product teardown, he was told: dissecting a competitor's stick to find out what was in it, and perhaps whether it was complying with the quality standards of the day.

Marlboro cigarettes had been introduced in the 1950s, a new kid on the block compared to some of his company's veteran brands. Its branding campaign was legendary, but the Marlboro Man wasn't the only reason the American-created brand was so popular. Marlboro was also one of the most distinct-tasting cigarettes in the world.

The lawyer watched the white-coat hunched over the counter, gently pulling away little strands and grains of tobacco from the cigarette with a tweezers, separating tobacco stem and pieces of golden leaf, and then examining the contents under a microscope.

One of the R & D team explained that they could figure out all of the ingredients in a Marlboro Light, but they couldn't make an exact duplicate of it—not without the recipe with the specific amounts of each ingredient. This wasn't cooking; it was baking.

It made the lawyer smile to think that even with all of their scientific resources, the R & D team still couldn't do it. That was the power of an original recipe.

The woman with tweezers looked up and asked the lawyer what his favourite brand of cigarette was. It was a clever question. Should he be honest?

"Vantage," he answered truthfully, even though it wasn't a brand the company made.

She nodded and disappeared into another room. A minute later she emerged with a pack of Vantage for him. She explained that the company had collected and organized pretty much every type of cigarette ever made; they'd built a living library of global tobacco brands.

In the good old days, R & D could have fun—relatively speaking—inventing new products and introducing "cool" new flavours, but those golden days of invention had ended. This was a sunset period now, no matter how much good cheer the team was mustering for his meeting.

Ultimately, he learned, during that visit, that R & D now spent most of its time contending scientifically with the reams of government regulations burdening the industry. The department was no longer really trying to live up to the twentieth-century corporate ambition of being "innovative" anymore; instead, R & D was extremely concerned about the issue of government compliance. If one word could sum up his R & D visit that day, it was definitely "compliance."

The lawyer remembered his teachers smoking in elementary school in the mid-1980s—in the staff room, with the door half-closed, the smell of cigarette smoke wafting down the hallway.

And he remembered the day his class was summoned to attend an all-school anti-smoking assembly, run by the school's nurse. Or was she a nurse? He doesn't actually recall what her official title was.

The school's entire student population had gathered in the gymnasium and sat quietly while the lights went down and the nurse showed them a slideshow of images of lungs that had been subjected to tar abuse. This was what the lungs of a long-term smoker looked like: unwholesome and webbed with darkness.

To help prove the point, the nurse had a machine on display. It was about the size of a person, and it had a "mouth." And around its mouth was a bizarre picture of this man—a generic white man, who wasn't particularly handsome. It was an intensely creepy-looking machine.

The whole school watched as the nurse unwrapped a pack of cigarettes, took the foil out, drew a cigarette out with her fingers, and put the cigarette in the mouth of the machine. They continued to watch as the machine smoked that cigarette right down to the filter, the smoke wafting through the school gym.

It was an educational event with some unintended consequences. The nurse had given a full demonstration of how to open a pack of cigarettes and how to smoke.

The point of the demonstration, of course, was to show the horror of what smoking a cigarette did to you. So, after the machine was done, the nurse reached inside its "body" and extracted a pad that had absorbed the smoke. She held it high above her and showed it to everyone.

See this pad, kids? She held it up as if it were the devil's baby. The pad was darkish yellow. This is what happens to your lungs, kids. Don't smoke.

The lawyer hadn't seen anything resembling that machine again, until now.

R & D possessed a smoking machine too, it turned out. Theirs sat alone in one of the old executive offices—almost as if it were management, peering out eerily from its large office window. This machine had about twenty "mouths" and no face. It wasn't designed to look human, although it was created to smoke as if it were. In its spacious, well-sealed and -ventilated office, it quietly smoked all day long, tabulating the results. It might as well have been called the vice-president of compliance.

The team could insert sticks as needed into one of the machine's many holes, and, simulating how lungs suck smoke, it would inhale. It measured what it breathed in and provided the team with yield levels of nicotine, tar, and carbon monoxide delivered from any particular brand of cigarette.

As anti-smoking attitudes hardened, government had been tackling the substance of the product itself, as well as the marketing efforts. And while the Master Settlement Agreement had been hammered out in the US during the late 1990s, in that same period the European Union was creating its own tobacco control measures.

The VP mentioned a term the lawyer had never heard of before: Directive General Five. The EU could dispense its authority in three ways: with a decision, a regulation, or a directive. A directive was an order, not a voluntary request.

It turned out that DG5 was the very unassuming name of a particular directive issued by the EU, and it was landing on the industry in the UK around this time.

The implications of DG5 were quite serious, the VP explained. It was specifically created to regulate the tobacco industry in Europe, and it ordered each government to direct tobacco companies to adhere to three specific implementations.

One: a global standard reducing the yields of tar, nicotine, and carbon monoxide—hence the machine in its own office smoking all day. To push the yields down demanded a major change in how the product was made, and this was passed on to R & D as a problem to solve.

Two: an end to the use of particular additives in their products. Again, this responsibility was passed on to R & D.

Three: larger health warnings on cigarette packages. This was in the marketing department's court to resolve, and it would be an expensive adjustment, since it meant redesigning every pack, in multiple languages, and adding new warnings in full colour. It added up to twenty-eight different packs that needed to be produced for twenty-five European countries—which meant hundreds of redesigned packages.

The lawyer came to understand why DG5 was weighing on the big brain of R & D.

It was all well and good for the EU to think a tobacco company could snap its fingers and produce a new cigarette that complied with these directives, but to do so the white-coats had to completely redesign the product inside and out within the new parameters.

This was the unseen side of tobacco regulation, and the changes couldn't happen overnight; they meant—in some cases—making alterations to intensely popular consumer products. Imagine if someone told Coca-Cola they had to add less corn syrup to their recipe, or McDonald's that it suddenly had to change the ingredients in its Big Mac sauce.

It was an absurd situation from the company's point of view. The all-important customer might have been 100 percent happy with the product, but the government was not. And so: remove flavours, remove potency, remove additives. And do it now.

Even when it came to the machine's measurement of the amount of tar, nicotine, and carbon monoxide being inhaled, it was complicated, he was informed, because there were major disagreements as to whether the machine actually mimicked how a human being smoked.

Some argued, for example, that what a cigarette delivered into the body could be manipulated by the behaviour of a smoker, which was why the machine's tabulations were a constant source of debate within the scientific and industry communities.

Did you have strong lungs and inhale deeply? Did you take long drags or short puffs? When you inhaled, did you cover the ventilation holes on the filter with your fingers? How many seconds did you wait between puffs? The lawyer thought about the way he smoked a cigarette.

This was just one puzzle R & D was faced with solving. The team patiently explained another dilemma to the lawyer: lowering tar and nicotine yields in the context of customer satisfaction, not just to meet EU requirements. They used alcohol as an example.

Let's say you drink your favourite brand of beer after work every day, and its label says it contains 5 percent alcohol. If you drink the contents of the bottle, there's no doubt about it—you will ingest 5 percent alcohol.

But what if suddenly the beer you always drank had its alcohol lowered to 3 percent. Would you stick to your one beer after work, or would you order two to compensate for the difference? Would the new product be acceptable? No one at the company knew the answer to these questions yet.

Nevertheless, tar, nicotine, and carbon monoxide "ceilings" were lowered, and this meant that every R & D department in every major tobacco company which possessed a machine—the VP of compliance—had to prove that each brand of cigarette was adhering to these rules.

The lawyer asked the team about an alternative reduced-risk product. Were they still trying to create a "safer" cigarette?

Yes, they'd spent years trying to create one, but to no avail.

"We've put a lot of resources into developing a safer product," said one senior member of the team. They'd lost a fortune so far, searching for the holy tobacco grail.

The irony, though, was that customers weren't asking for a safer product, even while continuing to purchase packs with increasingly large health warnings. As they conversed, the lawyer realized that one topic the team wasn't discussing with him was the actual health risk associated with the product: they were talking about compliance, not about the dangers of smoking or any issues related to addiction.

The lawyer asked a question about spiking cigarettes with nicotine, and they all looked at him strangely and went quiet. But one man did answer.

"Look, this is a legitimate operation. Don't believe everything you see on TV," he said, most likely referring to the 60 *Minutes* episode from 1996, which had focused on a different tobacco company and its R & D department.

Before his visit, the lawyer had imagined R & D as Q Division from James Bond films—that he'd walk into the lab and be dazzled by all sorts of zany designs and gadgets that were the future of the industry.

Instead, the many-mouthed machine sat in its outdated executive office, measuring out its days with an endless supply of cigarettes, looming over the department with a quiet authority—a reminder that the government was there in the R & D labs too, just not as easily identifiable as those customs officers in uniform safeguarding the taxable goods in the warehouse next door.

Something else the lawyer learned that afternoon: the basic design of cigarettes had remained the same for decades, but this popular product was continually changing, even while the all-important customer didn't want anything to change at all.

Change it up, but don't change a thing. These white-coated wizards had to accomplish both tasks, even though those goals seemed in total opposition to each other: a magic trick of sorts. Indeed, it seemed that the tobacco paradox had slipped through security and made itself at home in this research facility.

It turned out, when it came to tobacco regulation, there certainly were still troubles in Northern Ireland. As far as the lawyer could tell, the responsibility of government compliance had crushed and then neatly replaced the idea of innovation at the company.

A little light bulb winked on in his mind after his session with R & D.

The lawyer realized why the company had hired him into their legal department: his role would be to police his company in regards to the new government legislation and directives being aimed at tobacco products.

That new European Union directive loomed over the R & D department, and then it came to loom over his new professional life.

It turned out he wasn't going to be one of those lawyers who stood up in a courtroom and defended the industry. Instead, his duties would be about making sure his company—including all the employees he was meeting on this factory tour—adhered to every request in those damn directives. He would be preaching the importance of compliance and risk management. That's what became clear to him.

Still, he'd enjoyed the friendliness of the people he'd met. They were the true believers, and he thought about compliance issues as Madeleine drove him to the Galgorm Manor, the best hotel in the area.

After he got to his room, he went to the hotel restaurant for dinner. He sat at the bar and noticed quite a few company people there. For every cigarette he smoked, it seemed everyone else in the bar smoked two. And even though everyone had to be up at seven in the morning, for every drink he had, they had two, maybe three.

One of the guys at the bar asked if the lawyer had a girlfriend.

"Yes, I have a fiancée," he said.

"No, no," the man said. "Do you have a girlfriend here? If you come here a lot, you should."

So, this was part of his introduction to international business culture.

As he sipped his drink at the bar, he remembered proposing to his fiancée on a vacation in Florida. They had just finished dinner and were enjoying a bottle of wine on their hotel balcony, which overlooked the Gulf of Mexico.

He hadn't brought a ring with him. Instead, back in the room, when his girlfriend wasn't looking, he had written out a fake Air Canada boarding pass for a flight to Toronto, where the engagement ring would be waiting. It was a family heirloom, safely stored at his parents' house, a much nicer ring than he could afford.

That evening on the balcony, he reached into his pocket to make sure the handwritten boarding pass was still there. Then he smiled at his girlfriend, who was gazing out at the blood-orange sunset. She smiled back.

Then he said this to her: "In ten seconds, I'm going to get down on one knee and ask you to marry me. So you better start thinking . . ."

He pulled out the boarding pass and started to count down from ten out loud, excited to be asking, and nervous to hear her answer.

The warm memory insulated him in the foreign hotel bar.

He drained his drink and paid the bill. A few minutes later, he closed the door to his room. As he tried to fall asleep, he could hear some guy having sex with his "Irish girlfriend" in the room next door.

At the airport, he bought a bottle of perfume for his fiancée.

DRIVE TEAM

Back in London, Nancy kept his agenda updated and his tray of cigarettes full.

As Mary explained to the lawyer, a crucial aspect of his inductions was learning about how the company sold "sticks." This meant understanding as much as possible about the destinations of those thousands of cartons he'd seen stacked neatly in the factory warehouse.

During the next few weeks at HQ, the lawyer absorbed a massive amount of information in seminars from the sales managers about how sticks were sold—a continuation of his Tobacco University diploma. Sticks, he was told, belonged in the category of products called fast-moving consumer goods, or FMCGs.

Potato chips, pop, newspapers, bubble gum, and, yes, alcohol— these were all fast moving. Almost everything on a convenience store shelf was fast.

What was slow moving? Furniture, appliances, cars—big stuff, more expensive.

STICKS ARE
CIGARETTES

FIREBRAND

Tobacco sales were surging when he joined the company in 2001, despite the virulent and multiplying anti-smoking sentiment and government health warnings. Billions of sticks were being sold annually in the UK, and his company enjoyed 40 percent of those sales, ballpark.

The strategy with which sticks were sold was based on the company's deep knowledge of consumer behaviour and the available points of sale, or sales channels.

Thankfully, there were only four major sales channels in the domestic market to learn about, and according to his agenda the lawyer was being sent out again, this time on a local trip within London, to learn about the lowest rung of the sales force: the drive teams.

He didn't know what drive teams were.

Mary advised him to wear a suit for his field trip and said it would be an overnight expedition. The company wanted its new lawyer to get the full experience.

He went home that evening and informed his fiancée he'd be going on a sleepover. She was supportive. He picked out a sharp suit and tie, and he polished his shoes.

The next morning, a man called Ben was waiting in the parking area of HQ in a blue Vauxhall Vectra—a classic salesman's car.

"Hi, mate. You're coming with me," said Ben, who was lean and good-looking.

The lawyer got in on the passenger side.

He and Ben were roughly the same age: late twenties. After some opening chit-chat, his first impressions were: Ben was working-class, according to his accent and his suit, which wasn't nearly as nice as the lawyer's; Ben was friendly; Ben was chatty; Ben liked to smoke.

Ben had already lit up a cigarette, so the lawyer did too. As they drove into London, Ben out-smoked the lawyer two to one.

"So when did you join the company, mate?" Ben asked.

"I just joined," he answered.

"Are you working for Ian?

"Who's Ian?"

"He's my manager," Ben said, a little confused.

The information flowing to Ben seemed to be limited, and the lawyer decided to keep it that way. He didn't tell Ben who he was working for, and Ben didn't ask. It was clear that Ben had no idea he was taking out a management-level employee for an educational tour. In fact, Ben may have had the impression that his passenger was to be a new member of the drive team.

The lawyer had never spent a day with a guy like Ben. He'd been raised upper middle class in Toronto, had lived in a large house and attended expensive schools, and when he'd worked in journalism, it was in TV—the more glamorous sibling of print— and then he'd attended law school. He was privileged, and this was out of his zone.

They cruised into Southall, famous for its horrific rail accident in 1997 and full of apartment blocks and the convenience stores that served their residents. This was part of Ben's territory.

Bonus: the lawyer had never been to any of the neighbourhoods they visited that day. So this was kind of fun, a guided tour of a London he wasn't familiar with—and the family-owned convenience stores they were visiting made up an important proportion of sales for the tobacco business: more than a quarter, the lawyer had been told by the VP of sales.

It was Ben's job, as a member of the drive team, to hit a certain number of the convenience stores in his hunting ground each day. Who Ben was *not* dealing with: supermarkets, grocery store chains, or gas stations. His concern was solely independent convenience stores in this particular quadrant of London.

———

Here was the drill: Ben parked outside the store, went to the back of the car, and hoisted out his gym bag. Yes, he was that guy with the gym bag full of cigarettes.

These were his professional tools: gym bag and mobile phone. His office cubicle was the car, as far as the lawyer could tell. In the bag, Ben had cartons of sticks, yes, but also paraphernalia: branded lighters, replacement advertising, bulbs for light boxes that flashed the brand.

Ben locked the car and headed towards the store with the bag. The lawyer wished he had worn a less impressive suit and not polished his shoes, which were gleaming.

This was a predominantly South Asian, working-class neighbourhood of London. Ben was white, the lawyer was white, and they were wearing suits. When they exited the car, the corporate aura emanating from their suits didn't match the neighbourhood vibe. The lawyer felt like a narc.

He followed Ben into the convenience store.

The proprietors of the store—a husband and wife—were sitting behind the cash register, and as the lawyer quickly saw, Ben treated them as if they were king and queen of this kingdom of fast-moving consumer goods.

The lawyer scanned the store. It was sort of rundown and poorly lit compared to a supermarket. The shelves were a little crooked but well stocked with gifts, canned food, tea, soft drinks, chocolate bars, rice, curry sauces, onions, and a couple of varieties of vegetable he'd never seen before.

The king and queen knew who Ben was before he'd said a word, and it became obvious, quickly, that they had no love for him. It was the expressions on their faces: when they saw Ben, their eyes went dead.

"Hi, mate," Ben said to the king.

Ben was chipper. He didn't introduce the lawyer. But it didn't matter how chipper Ben acted; the owners looked at him as if he were the scum of the Earth.

Most owners they dealt with looked at Ben the same way.

This was interesting to the lawyer, considering Ben was about to offer bargain deals on cartons of cigarettes and was a jovial guy. The shopkeepers, though, knew that behind Ben's wall of chipperness, he was a corporate land predator representing a powerful business empire.

As for the lawyer, the owners didn't even look at him. He was perceived as Ben's assistant.

The lawyer scanned the shelf behind the counter. Independent convenience stores like these kept only about ten half-cartons of sticks on their shelves, and this meant it was an extremely competitive space.

Why would such stores keep such a limited number of sticks in stock? Because of crime: the threat of burglary or robbery.

If you're going to burglarize a convenience store, you're not going to steal chocolate bars or chewing gum, or onions. You're going to steal cash and you're going to steal cigarettes. Cigarettes were valuable, light to carry, and easy to sell on the black market—out of a gym bag like Ben's.

That made Ben an important part of this king and queen's consumer ecosystem. He came directly to the shopkeeper, and though they didn't like him very much, they'd deal with him. Ben was convenient to convenience stores; he delivered an important product straight into their kingdom.

To make matters more complex, these convenience store owners didn't make much profit from cigarettes. They sold tobacco products because people who bought cigarettes might buy other things: candy, newspapers, cola, the fast-moving consumer goods with higher margins.

It was a business model based on consumer addiction. If you had a high number of smokers living in your neighbourhood, you lured them in by selling them their preferred brands, and then, hopefully, other products as well.

From that perspective, Ben was crucial to this consumer circle of life, especially for an independent convenience store struggling to keep customers coming through that door, competing with slick and plentiful commercial grocery stores, which bought in larger quantities and could therefore sell products at lower prices.

Watching Ben work, the lawyer was learning why these mom-and-pop convenience stores were so important, and vulnerable, to drive teams: there were no planograms.

If you were a committed smoker, and you were smart, you were not buying your cigarettes here. You were getting them at the most important point of sale for tobacco companies: supermarkets.

There was a reason they were called "super": they were large; they were organized; and they were cheap. The supers saved you time, and they saved you money.

You didn't go to a supermarket to buy one can of cola; you bought a case of it. If you smoked, you visited a supermarket for your weekly or monthly supply of sticks.

The lawyer remembered being shown an astounding figure when he started at the company: one of every eleven pounds spent in the UK was spent at a Tesco, the largest grocery chain in the country.

The supers were well aware of the value they provided, and they were highly organized to squeeze as much money as possible out of each company supplying them with product. To do this in the most efficient way, the executive teams at the supers had implemented a system called a planogram to keep track of their precious retail space.

What was a planogram? A detailed map measuring every last inch of shelf space in each supermarket. Legend had it that Kmart had invented planograms in the 1980s to precisely map out any given store's retail space, and the idea spread quickly across retail empires.

A planogram dictated exactly where a product could be placed, whether it was at eye level, on the top shelf, or way down there at the bottom or at the farthest end of the aisle from the checkout, where fewer shoppers would see it.

Just as vital, planograms showed company reps exactly where their product was being placed in comparison to their competition.

Maybe you thought that the location of each product was up to the shelf stocker? No, it was not. Supers carried a full selection of cigarettes maintained by the stock-keeping unit algorithm, in retail jargon the SKU. It was the SKU computer program that tracked every product and dictated to human workers exactly where a product should go: an all-knowing eye-keeping watch.

The product didn't just magically appear on the shelf. In a commercial grocery store, no fast-moving consumer good ever got displayed and sold without a representative who negotiated with and paid money to the supermarket chain for renting shelf space through a planogram system.

This was "pay to play," and the planogram became an almost universal system used by corporate grocery stores around the planet.

The lawyer's company, he learned, had a team of reps and managers to oversee the planogramming of it all: negotiating agreements, haggling over planogram pricing, and greenlighting special promotions when possible (and where tobacco promotion was still legal).

If the tobacco company wanted a carton of cigarettes placed up front in the aisle, facing the customer at the beginning of the cigarette section, they paid for it.

It was expensive but worth it, he learned. You received exactly what you payed for and there was no way of gaming the system. This sophistication behind the placement of tobacco products at the supers was the same as for toothpaste, cereals, or colas.

Still, most people who drank Coke didn't go and buy Pepsi because it was more prominently displayed. They bought only Coke. So despite the premiums for eye-level or front-of-aisle placement, the truth was most consumers remained loyal to their chosen brand for their entire lives and went hunting for that brand when shopping.

With brand loyalty so firm, you might wonder how supers remained a competitive arena for the companies' sales teams. Actually, there were very few competitive advantages at the supers compared to those at the convenience kingdoms Ben and the lawyer were visiting that day.

"Good news!"

Ben started his pitch to the owners, turning the charm up.

He gave the owners a spiel about a promotion being done for a major American brand of cigarettes that was not popular in the UK.

He pulled out of his magic bag a carton of cigarettes. He held the carton up in front of them as if it were a bar of gold. It would be easier on Ben if he were offering the most popular brands that the company manufactured — but he wasn't.

Ben didn't push any of the famous brands — or the luxury brands — because those basically sold themselves. Ben's particular boulder to push was to hawk brands that weren't doing well. He was pushing product into these stores that nobody wanted to buy, so there was a bit of a *Glengarry Glen Ross* feel to his routine. He was selling swampland.

Ben's special offer: "Buy one carton of these spectacular cigarettes at retail price, and you get the second carton *for free!*"

Good offer, thought the lawyer. An offer that was difficult to say no to.

"But there's more!" Ben said.

He pulled out more offerings from his magic bag: a bunch of lighters, light boxes, and other signage. He'd throw in all this advertising paraphernalia (crap, really) for a steal!

The lighters were useful to the owners, though. They could give them away to valued customers to build goodwill, or they could sell them at a profit. And they could put all this signage up on their already crowded counter, which would help sell these new brands they'd purchased for a deep discount from Ben.

The special deal, the hundred-watt smile, and the freebies: they were a means to an end for Ben. Just like in the supers, this was a war of inches. Inches of shelf space, and inches of countertop next to the cash register.

Ben's agenda seemed fairly direct. He wanted his brands at eye level on that shelf behind the owners, and he wanted to place his company's advertising on the counter in front of them: lighters, light boxes, placards.

He was a fast negotiator and quickly struck a deal on the cartons and free lighters. In exchange, there was another component to the bargain: Ben would be allowed to physically get behind their counter. The lawyer watched as king and queen moved aside and allowed Ben access to their sanctum.

Ben took his jacket off, rolled up his sleeves, and for the next two minutes became the old-fashioned stock boy, moving packs around very quickly on the shelf like a sleight-of-hand magician.

The lawyer immediately saw the value of the transaction. Ben's behaviour simply wouldn't be possible at the supers. Here, though, there was no SKU program to be alerted to his activity. Ben was rearranging the shelves so his company's brands were all directly in front of the customer, at eye level, as they paid at the register.

Was it crazy to believe that simply moving tobacco products from one part of the shelf to another was going to change a customer's buying habits?

No, the lawyer was learning, it was not crazy at all. Because even brand-loyal consumers asked themselves at least three basic questions during their moment of decision: What is directly in front of me? What is easiest to buy? What is cheapest to buy?

Jill or Joe Smoker might look behind the counter at eye level, spy a brand they didn't recognize, and ask, "How much is that?" The lawyer thought about the randomness with which he'd bought his first pack of cigarettes, based on an advertisement that caught his eye on a countertop.

Another possibility: Jill or Joe Smoker might see the attractive sale price on the light box and go for it. "I'll just take one of those."

Ben's efforts provided the company with a slight edge over its competitors by placing their product at eye level, moving the competitor's products away from that position, and placing as many ads as he could between the counter and the tobacco shelves—and into the direct path of the customer's gaze for a few seconds of their busy day.

Ben had finished. The entire process of striking a deal and rearranging this one convenience kingdom had taken him less than ten minutes. At the end of the process, the king made the payment in cash, which Ben accepted and tucked quickly into his pocket.

"Goodbye, mate! See you soon!" he said to the king.

The lawyer followed Ben out the door, back to Ben's office: the Vauxhall.

Inside the car, Ben made a few scribbles on a list, then lit up a smoke. They sailed on to the next convenience kingdom on his list.

The lawyer wondered if Ben was skimming product, because when Ben ran out of cigarettes, he just reached into the back seat, took a couple of packs, and chucked one to the lawyer. Or maybe this was a perk of the job, the same way those factory workers got free cigarettes on their breaks every day and his tray was filled each morning?

For lunch they went for Indian. It was better than any Indian food he'd ever had—dishes with spices he'd never tasted. Later, its heat made his gastrointestinal system melt down, which meant, unfortunately, he also had the chance to tour a number of convenience store washrooms. The state of those washrooms you don't want to know about.

Then they filled up at a gas station.

Gas station convenience stores were the next rung up among those four sales channels the lawyer had learned so much about. They were blandly called the convenience store channel, even though they were gas stations. This may have been because, when the automobile took over, convenience stores multiplied along with gas stations.

If supers were like big-box bookstores, and mom-and-pop convenience kingdoms were like indie booksellers, gas station stores were more like airport bookstores; they didn't have everything, but what they stocked were the winners, those brands that were most popular and would fly off the shelves, like *New York Times* bestsellers and Oprah's Book Club picks.

Gas station counters were pay to play and planograms again, but in even stronger favour of the vendor. In this arena, unlike in the supers, smokers tended to buy only one pack at a time. And in this tightly organized commercial environment, tobacco companies rented space by the pack, not the carton or shelf. The vendors could charge a premium for that space, and both vendor and tobacco company made a decent profit on the sale of each pack.

Everybody won.

The lawyer and Ben pushed on to more kingdoms, and at each visit the lawyer observed that Ben was very good at his job.

His skill set: personable, persistent, swift. Ben had learned which lines he could cross, and which he could not, in each kingdom they visited that day. Every proprietor had slightly different laws in their land, and it seemed like Ben knew them all by heart.

He was a front-line soldier in a turf war to get the company's brands on the shelves, and as the lawyer learned, there were other soldiers prowling in these consumer trenches too.

Later that afternoon, Ben pulled up at a store but did not rush in as he usually did.

"Wait, I know that car," he said, sort of excited.

It was the rep from Rothmans.

While the competing rep was in the store, they sat and smoked, like detectives in a B-movie stakeout. After a few minutes, they watched as the Rothmans guy exited the store with his gym bag, got into his car, and drove off to his next target. Then Ben moved in.

Inside this kingdom, all the Rothmans products had been freshly moved and were at eye level.

Ben unzipped his gym bag, turned on the charm, and gave a superb sales pitch. The owners gave him the dead eyes and played along—even though they had literally just endured the same spiel from another rep.

Then Ben used another negotiation tactic in his arsenal, and a devastating one for the competition: the pack swap. Ben was determined. This was war.

"You give me the competitor's cigarettes, say ten packs, and I'll give you another twenty packs, for free," he said. This was one of Ben's most aggressive offers, and it was in the kingdom's favour, so it was accepted.

While Ben was going from store to store, there were sales reps from other tobacco companies doing the same thing. All day, all week, competitors were working to undo all of Ben's accomplishments, just as Ben was working to undo theirs. Tobacco drive teams were racing all over London with gym bags full of sticks, getting behind convenience store counters and rearranging everything.

It was madness, the myth of Sisyphus meets the Muppets, the lawyer thought. But if the others were doing it, they had to do it too, he guessed. Ben was a foot soldier for the company, doing the tough sales work that needed to be done.

Over the course of that day, the lawyer followed Ben on between ten and fifteen store visits as he rearranged eye-level branding across the countertops of London convenience kingdoms. And then they went to meet Ben's boss to report on their deeds.

It was about seven o'clock and getting dark. The street lights and marquee signs were winking to life as they parked at their last stop: a Posthouse hotel.

The hotel wasn't in Ben's territory, but it was where the foreman wanted them at the end of each shift. About half a dozen drive teams from around London were gathering here at dusk, at the hotel pub, to report in to their boss.

If the blue Vauxhall was Ben's cubicle, then this hotel was the boardroom. The lawyer had never stayed at a Posthouse before, the UK version of a Holiday Inn.

Ben went into the back of the car, retrieved a package of cash and the lists he'd been scribbling all day. Then they went into the hotel and straight to the bar.

The room was smoky. They sat down at a long table in the bar with the other drive team members. The reps were mostly men, but not exclusively. Besides Ben, there were another eight reps, and the lawyer noted that the women were pretty and the men handsome.

The manager's name was Ian, and he sat at a different table nearby.

Ian was older and wore a leather jacket. He smoked a lot, and he had a drink in front of him. Ian seemed to know that the lawyer should be there but didn't hint that he knew he was management.

In minute detail, Ian interviewed each sales rep about their day. While he fired off questions, he was taking cash and doing inventory. The lawyer watched this process and wondered what kind of business this was. Was Ben even technically an employee of the company?

When it was Ben's turn to be debriefed, the lawyer sat nearby—which Ian noted.

"How was your day?" Ian asked the lawyer, almost without looking at him.

"Okay," he answered.

Ian nodded. That was the totality of their exchange.

Ian then focused on Ben. They chatted about which stores took what inventory, whether Ben had sold everything needed, how the competitor landscape was looking, whether he'd bumped into any competing reps. Ben counted out £600 on the table, and Ian took the money off the table. Then Ben turned to the lawyer.

"My day is done," he said with a smile.

Ian did not give Ben any cash back.

He gave each member of the drive team the following: a key for a room at the hotel, a free dinner in the restaurant, and vouchers for two pints of beer. If they wanted more than two drinks, they had to pay for it themselves. This was raw England—smoking, football, drinks, and cash business.

Being a drive team member was nobody's dream job, but they were all working towards a target for the week. Whoever pushed the most product into a store was given a prize. What was the prize? You guessed it: more free smokes. They all smoked.

The two free beers vanished pretty quickly.

One of the women was eyeing the lawyer.

"So, you just joined the company?" she asked him.

"Yes," he said.

"Where did you work before?"

"In London."

"I bet he's here to spy on us," she said to the group.

He nodded and gave her a smile. "Yeah, right."

The lawyer drank his free beer and scanned the crowd at the bar.

Bars were part of the fourth sales channel for the company, which had a really uncatchy acronym: HORECA. It stood for hotels, restaurants, and cafés, but it also represented train stations, airports, nightclubs, golf clubs, bowling alleys, and anywhere else that wasn't a chain store or convenience store. The bar in this hotel was a perfect example.

There were two kinds of sales to consider when studying up on HORECA, as the lawyer had been doing: the sale of a single pack through a person, usually behind a bar, and the sale of a single pack through a machine.

Fact: nobody ever planned on buying cigarettes from a bartender or machine. Either way, you were getting ripped off.

You've seen it a million times: there's the bartender, and the bartender has a little container with a small selection of brands hidden under the bar—not very many kinds, and probably not your preferred brand. The bartender would smile and charge you a small fortune to buy one of those packs. This was why a sale through HORECA was called "a distressed purchase."

The entire sales channel was based on consumer desperation. You bought smokes this way because it was cold out, or you were in the middle of breaking up with your significant other, or your friend was having a nervous breakdown and crying into a vodka shot, or you had your eye on someone at the bar and didn't want to go just yet, or you were so drunk you couldn't make it out the door to get them somewhere cheaper.

Then you spied that wonderful little machine with its inviting lights glowing in a dark corner, and those magical little packs floating behind the lit-up plastic case. The night was saved! You didn't have to leave! You could buy smokes from the machine!

Maybe it was easier, psychologically, being ripped off by a machine.

At the vending machine, you might notice that the price was rounded up to the nearest whole number, and that the packs inside had been specially manufactured to provide a higher profit margin to the owner of said machine: a more expensive pack with fewer cigarettes.

Yes, there were vending machine empires, and these companies did well, because you were lazy, you had not planned ahead, and when it was late and you were tired, you would pay more.

You couldn't negotiate or argue with a machine; you made a choice. That was why the machines were genius. The establishments giving them space were making money; the owners of the machines were making money; and the cigarette company was making money. All because it wasn't convenient to leave. This wasn't pay to play; it was pay to stay.

The lawyer looked around at this crew of drive team colleagues, and he wondered how well any of them—including Ian—were educated in the company's overall sales strategies.

Ben knew his routine, his piece of the puzzle, but he certainly hadn't been given a tour of the factory in Northern Ireland or briefed by R & D. Instead, Monday to Thursday, he and this crew were hawking sticks out of gym bags and staying at a Posthouse hotel.

The lawyer, on the other hand, was being given inductions with high-level management, who were discussing billions of dollars in sales, and now he was watching one guy pushing £600 across a pub table to another guy. The little calculator in his mind was clicking:

there was the cost of the goods, the time, the gas, the lunch, the hotel room, the free dinner and drinks, and the management of it all.

This team hasn't even sold that many cigarettes, and yet the company was buying them dinner and paying for a hotel room. How were they making any money off this system? Why was so much effort being spent on selling these lesser brands to kings and queens of convenience kingdoms across London?

This was about far more than the money, the lawyer decided; it was about influence, about commanding every last inch of influence over customers still available.

Ben came knocking on the lawyer's door early the next morning.

They were on the road by 6 A.M., and there was no breakfast included at the hotel. Instead, they stopped for coffee at a gas station, and around lunchtime Ben dropped him back at head office.

"Good luck in whatever it is that you're doing," Ben said. And then, "Goodbye, mate."

The lawyer waved goodbye to Ben, and he never saw him again.

VOWS ARE MADE

The lawyer's fiancée:

She'd practically grown up on an airplane—a lot of smiles and free biscuits from the airline attendants, a cockpit visit, a shining little metal airplane with branded wings as a souvenir for the brave young traveller.

Her mother was London-born but had worked as a journalist across the United States, Europe, and Asia. Her father was an executive in a global market-research firm and had been based in far-flung places: Borneo, Thailand, and then Hong Kong, where her parents were married and where she was born.

She had told the lawyer about her earliest memories of her dad: in the kitchen, smoking cigars with his coffee and newspaper. He was a heavy smoker, and travelled frequently, all year round. He was hardly home, which was probably why her mom stopped working, to take care of their baby daughter.

Life in Hong Kong brought early exposure to different cultures, languages, and flavours. When the family relocated to London, her parents insisted she attend a French school; they were both fluent in multiple languages, although sometimes it wasn't clear to her that they spoke the same language. There were lots of fights, and even in silence she could sense the tension radiating.

A few years later, it was back to Hong Kong, where she was home-schooled by her stay-at-home mother and often waved goodbye to her dad on his way out the door.

Soon the family pushed on to Bangkok, and then to Singapore, before they boomeranged back to England, which in her teenage years became more of a home to her than Hong Kong.

Her mother didn't like being back in London, though, so they moved again—this time to Rome.

She attended international school, learned Italian, got lost in the churches, museums, and piazzas. She made new friends—the sons and daughters of diplomats and expat execs—and they wandered the ancient streets, a little global gang of outsiders. They threw coins into the Trevi Fountain, flirted with young Italians, made fun of tourists, loitered in archways older than Christ, and treaded over the chipped relics of Western civilization in their designer leather shoes or Superga running shoes, depending on the weather.

She was inspired by the deepness of this culture, leaning in to it at every turn, and it seeped into her soul in unexpected ways. Perhaps that's why she chose to study art history at the American University of Paris and the Sorbonne. She even managed to find an internship at the Louvre, where she helped conduct research for one of the world's leading historical wallpaper experts. Old wallpaper aside, to walk the banks of the Seine at sunset or party with friends in the oily lamplight of cobblestoned courtyards sometimes felt like living inside a masterpiece.

Her father was half Canadian, the lawyer had been pleasantly surprised to learn, and over one summer she decided to change her surroundings completely and crossed the Atlantic to Toronto. She had cousins there. For a time, she worked a job at a call centre, spending her days surveying Canadians by phone on any manner of odd subjects. She rented a room at Massey College, at the University of Toronto. It was idyllic, but she was lonely phoning strange Canadians and eating solo on restaurant patios.

Then she migrated south to New York, loved the electricity of the place, but eventually wound up gravitating back to London, where she worked for a magazine called *Metal Bulletin*, a metal manufacturing publication. Bonus: part of her job was travelling to remote Italian cities and villages, selling ad space to European metal barons.

She'd become her parents' daughter: a world wanderer, finding she could always fit in but never quite feeling at home. The kinetic adventure was always interesting, but it wasn't always easy. She longed for a home she'd never had; she'd have to build one for herself, she came to realize. Alone?

It was around that time, while working in London, that she and the lawyer collided. By that point, she was hanging out with a woman who worked at NBC Europe. One night, she found herself out at a pub with the NBC crew, including a young man who had previously worked at the broadcasting company but was now finishing law school.

He had a smile in his eyes as he smoked his cigarette. As the last person to join the group, she asked if anyone needed a drink. He answered without hesitating, "I'll have a double whisky." She was initially not impressed, but she brought him over his double.

Oddly, the two hit it off, and over the evening they traded questions and barbs. Wow, was he smart. Wow, was he charming. She pointed out to him he had an innocent, baby-face complexion, which probably meant he could get away with anything. They both laughed. Soon they moved in together.

Later, when he was being courted by a Big Tobacco company, she was as fascinated as he was by the prospect of him working for them.

She didn't smoke, but he did. She didn't seem to mind.

Most of her friends smoked, and she'd grown up with a chimney —her dad. So, she encouraged him to explore, and then to accept, the role. It was a step up for him professionally, and for them as a couple. The duo became popular figures at dinner parties: everyone wanted to know more about the tobacco industry, while puffing away the evening.

The challenge now: he was being asked to travel more often on company business. Maybe because she'd grown up in a family where her mother had resented her father's being constantly in the skies, she vowed not to repeat that pattern.

The lawyer was blown away by her attitude towards his frequent flying. If doors opened, you should walk through them, she told him. Take the opportunities that presented themselves. To explore new countries, and to experience other cultures, was a deep privilege. She'd joined that club as a young girl and was happy for him to become a member: Club World.

She wanted to support him, and encourage opportunities for their family to progress and grow. When he said he was off to Northern Ireland, or Spain, or France, or Switzerland, or wherever, she helped him pack and made sure he felt prepared.

She did wish, though, that he wouldn't smoke so much. Now that he was actually working for a tobacco company, it was more complicated to ask him to cut down.

The night of her bachelorette party, he waved goodbye from the door. She stayed out with her friends until dawn: what happens in sleazy London nightclubs, stays in sleazy London nightclubs . . . It was a fun and wild night, and she couldn't recall, exactly, how or when she arrived home. And she really did feel at home, here, with him. Perhaps for the first time in her life.

What wasn't fun was when he woke her up later that morning and reminded her his company garden party was beginning in two hours. "Fine, honey, fine, just give me a second, okay?"

She'd made a promise to herself and her fiancé to support him in his new role at the company—so she honoured that promise, even though she was practically blind from the booze still oozing through her system, and the crushing headache.

The summer party for the legal department unfolded in one of those expansive English backyards with a trimmed lawn, an orchard, and a swimming pool. This world of privilege was the home of the company's general counsel.

The lawyer reported to Mary; Mary reported to general counsel; and the general, who ruled the legal department, reported directly to the company's CEO.

The company didn't say you had to be at the party, but you had to be there.

In a very English, upper-middle-class way, it was a chance for the lawyer and his wife-to-be to meet his new colleagues in a more relaxed, informal setting distinctly outside the office.

At some point early on that afternoon, his fiancée let it slip that she'd been out at her "hen night," and everyone seemed to find that very funny. They were the special couple, embarking on a life together, and the company was a part of that journey now. He watched his fiancée describe in hushed tones to a few wives what had transpired the previous night and heard excited cackles from across the lawn.

The legal team was a family oriented department; everybody had a partner, wife, or husband. Most of them had kids. Children ran around the big, sunny lawn, and the hosts had rented a clown for the afternoon. He doesn't remember if the clown smoked, but one of the personal assistants had taken the time to bring a large selection of company tobacco to ensure there was plenty available. There was also a bar, stocked with premium alcohol, and, of course, an exquisite meal, served outdoors.

About fifty people were there; the legal department was an intimate, exclusive club within the company.

The general counsel sat at a table with his wife, and both of them smoked.

It was up to each couple to visit the general's table and talk to them — to show homage and give thanks. This was for a good reason: general counsel knew the company in a way few people did. He had been a lawyer there for thirty years, and was about seven feet tall — no joke. His wife was a gracious co-host, with a bright smile, and dripping in jewels, at an afternoon garden party!

General counsel always smoked a pipe, and when he wasn't smoking his pipe, he kept it in his pocket. It wasn't unusual to spy his tall shape strolling the halls at the office with smoke rising out of his trouser pocket. At restaurants with him, you didn't order wine, and you didn't pay the bill. You waited for the general to order the wine, and you waited for him to pick up the bill when it arrived.

When there was an opening, the lawyer and his fiancée walked to the general's table and sat down. Everyone was introduced, and it was going well until the lawyer made a serious faux pas.

He pulled out his pack of Peter Stuyvesant cigarettes and pulled one out to light it. He'd bought them at his local convenience store, and he knew enough not to take them into the office with him, but here it had slipped his mind. He just wasn't thinking.

When he took the pack out and placed it on the table, the general noticed immediately.

"Get that off the table," he said quietly.

"Why?" the lawyer laughed, lighting his cigarette.

A beat of silence passed.

"I'm not going to tell you again. Get it off the table!" the general barked.

The lawyer pulled the pack off the table, suddenly feeling like an inexperienced junior who hadn't learned to play by the rules yet.

It was never mentioned again, and he knew never to do it again. It was a long time before he purchased a competitor's brand.

The point: no one was kidding around here. This company made only tobacco products, and it was the largest tobacco company in the UK. Their brands were as well known in the UK as Heinz or Coke. And there was one goal: to manufacture as many sticks as possible, and to sell as many of them as they could.

Another exchange he had that afternoon was with Serious Bob, a senior lawyer at the company. Serious Bob was about as square as a person could get, as his office nickname implied.

The lawyer and Bob were smoking and chatting just off behind some bushes near the edge of the lawn when Bob's wife suddenly came into view, ambling towards them in the sparkling sunlight. With no warning, Bob threw his cigarette into the lawyer's hands. Now he had two cigarettes! So he smoked Bob's as well.

When Bob's wife wandered on to another group, the lawyer smiled at his colleague quizzically.

"Dude, does your wife not know that you smoke?"

"She doesn't."

The lawyer laughed. "How is that possible?"

"It's easy. I just say I've been sitting in meetings with you all day."

This was a person who probably never cheated on his wife, who was an excellent lawyer, and a family man, but his wife didn't know he smoked. It was almost as if Bob was having an affair with cigarettes.

Serious Bob fell into the growing category of "secret smoker" — and there were more and more of these phantom smokers. They came out of hiding at parties, lingered on street corners in front of bars, lurking just outside whatever social gathering they were part of, searching for their fix. They were a trending subcategory of smoker who couldn't face the public shame of lighting up in front of friends and family.

The general counsel was due to retire, and there were two contenders for his position: Mary, the lawyer's superior, and Simon, both group legal counsels. One of those two was to be anointed the new head of the legal department. It was a group board position — a master of the universe kind of job.

Mary was the hard-working Type A, battling sexism and chauvinism in the industry while raising a family. She wanted the position. Unfortunately, there was a deep macho culture at the company and it was still a business dominated by men. Other than marketing and HR, women were usually secretaries and assistants.

This was to the lawyer's advantage.

He was instantly supported by a lot of the old guard simply because he was young and male. Some of the most senior men at the company wanted to show him the rules of the game and push him up the ladder.

Early in his induction phase, he was invited to attend an International Council meeting. Within the industry, this gathering of senior lawyers from across multiple tobacco companies was known as the "merchants of death" meeting.

He was not attending as a lead lawyer, though, and he wasn't sure why he was asked to be there at all. It was another "sit and listen, kid" experience.

The meeting was held annually, but it rotated to a different location each year: Rome, New York, London, Madrid. That year, it was held in cobblestoned, canalled Amsterdam, and after the official meeting, a smaller crew of tobacco lawyers stayed up late, drinking very expensive Scotch and smoking Cuban cigars. He was invited to join them and discovered they were a liver-hardened bunch; he drank until the world went crooked and dimmed.

The next morning, he awoke in a deep mental fog. He stumbled down to the lobby to check out of the hotel and was presented with his room bill by the concierge. His head still hurt from all the Scotch he'd drowned in. He stared down at the blurry number at the bottom of his bill until it came into focus. And suddenly he felt terrified.

The bill he was being asked to pay was for thousands of euros.

The lawyer scanned the line items, trying to understand what the charges were for. Then it clicked. The entire membership of the "merchants of death" after-party had charged their cigars and all of that wonderful Scotch to his room.

He didn't know what to do—so he called general counsel, who picked up the phone.

"Welcome to the tobacco industry," the general boomed. "Don't be the first to go to bed."

After that garden party, the lawyer really felt as if he and his fiancée were being accepted as part of the company family. It had that *Godfather*-like feeling to it. You're one of us now.

During lunch the next week, his colleagues asked him for details about his upcoming wedding.

The ceremony was in London, and then the couple were jetting to the Seychelles for their honeymoon. The timing of the wedding was slightly awkward. He had joined the department just weeks before the event and so wasn't close enough to any of his new colleagues to consider inviting them.

Lunch, by the way, may have been the most important part of his workday in those early days at the company, because it afforded him time to chat with his colleagues on his team.

They were offered a three-course meal in the dining room, where the surroundings were more akin to a golf club than a boring suburban office canteen. And there was, of course, a seating hierarchy. Managers sat with managers; personal assistants with personal assistants; lawyers with lawyers. Everyone would take the full hour for lunch, including coffee and cigarettes to finish.

Even though not a single one of his colleagues would be a guest at the wedding, the team seemed determined to show its support for the new lawyer and his fiancée. The general even succeeded in holding a formal dinner in honour of the couple, which included all the lawyers on his team, just one week before they tied the knot. No expense was spared, and there was a speech from general counsel, pipe in hand.

"It's not every day that we have a wedding in the legal department . . ." the general boomed.

It was like that. They were being taken care of. The lawyer and bride-to-be were floored by the friendliness and sincerity of the company, one he had joined less than two months earlier.

At the end of the dinner, the general presented the couple with a gift basket and a generous voucher for an upscale department store. He'd been granted three weeks paid vacation for the wedding and honeymoon.

Their wedding took place on a sparkling early September afternoon.

The couple exchanged vows, were joined in matrimony, kissed, and then partied with their friends and family.

One of his groomsmen made a speech that introduced the lawyer as a "tobacco baron." Everyone laughed.

The groomsman was educated at Eton—as were Prince William and Prince Harry—and the Old Etonian was currently working as a highly ranked private secretary in the British government. For many years thereafter, his groomsman would give the lawyer a hard time about being employed by the tobacco industry. Whenever they went to a restaurant together, this friend always made sure never to allow the lawyer to pay—fine—for fear of accepting money from Big Tobacco.

The day after the wedding, the lawyer and his wife boarded a plane and flew economy class to Mahé, one of the secluded Seychelles islands, which hover on the Indian Ocean, east of Africa.

The Seychelles were a world away, a floating bubble of luxurious resorts and pristine beaches that were all the rage, and practically a rite of passage, among upper-middle-class British honeymooners. It seemed like almost everyone on the plane was a newlywed couple glowing with possibility.

The honeymoon was not cheap, mind you, and they'd saved up for two years to afford the trip.

They checked into paradise as "Mr. and Mrs." and were led to their honeymoon suite: a private villa with two levels capped by an intricate thatched roof. They explored the spacious mezzanine and living room and climbed the staircase to their bedroom nest. The "wow" feature was the double doors off the living room that opened onto a stone terrace with a beachfront view of the Indian Ocean. Sail a few hundred kilometres northwest and you'd hit Somalia, headquarters of the real international pirates.

That evening, they had dinner, toasted their future together, listened to the ocean rollers, and felt the breeze wash over them. The next morning, they strolled down to the beach, allowed their vitamin-D-starved UK skin to absorb the healing rays of sunshine, and felt like dolphins playing in the frothing waves.

A few hours later, they returned to the villa, discarding their sandy bathing suits on the floor. She disappeared into the shower, and he kicked back and turned on the news, just for a second.

On CNN, a reporter was standing on a rooftop in New York City. Looming in the distance behind the reporter was a massive plume of black smoke rising from the World Trade Center. The lawyer could see only one of the two towers, and at first he thought it was just smoke obscuring the camera's view of the other tower.

When his bride emerged from the steamy washroom, he explained that all hell was breaking loose in the US and it seemed as if the country was under attack.

They sat together, glued to the shocking images on their television. And as the reporter on the rooftop continued to update viewers, the man suddenly turned away from the camera as if beckoned by someone calling his name. Behind him, the hulking, smouldering tower disintegrated in front of their eyes, falling into a horrible shroud of dark smoke and leaving a serene slice of hazy blue sky where it once stood. The second tower was simply gone.

The CNN reporter turned back to the camera and uttered the sentence that so many remembered from that world-changing moment: "Good Lord . . . there are no words . . ."

Outside their terrace doors, their own reality was suddenly jarring. It was the opposite of what they saw on the television screen. The ocean glimmered and winked at them.

As the TV camera angled down to street level, it looked as if the entirety of New York City was being swallowed by smoke. The lawyer sat in paradise with his new bride, chain-smoked, and watched as the world on television turn to ash.

Over the next few days, the lawyer and his wife contacted as many of their family and friends as possible. They had colleagues who worked near the Twin Towers. Messages were left on voicemail: "Hi, we wanted to call and make sure you're okay. Here's the fax number of our hotel."

Each afternoon, they'd return from their dolphin swims to find faxes slipped under their door, replies from friends across the world, with messages like "We're okay. We love you." The company also sent him a fax saying they hoped the couple were safe.

The magnitude of what had occurred didn't hit until their honeymoon was over and they journeyed home.

They flew economy class through Dubai, where airport security was on steroids. Machine guns were cradled in the arms of stone-faced sentinels guarding international borders. The lawyer was repeatedly stopped and taken aside for questioning by different security personnel while his wife watched. "Where are you going? Why are you here? What's the purpose of your travel? Where were you born? Where do you live? What do you do in your professional life?"

The lawyer answered these questions as best he could. The couple were permitted to return home to begin their new life together.

For a short time after they returned to London, the lawyer was given the job of being the legal department liaison to the company's consumer services department.

Consumer services received correspondence from consumers, and he helped handle their queries. These were mostly letters, but there was also a phone number consumers could call. This was 2001, so there was no widespread use of email quite yet.

The legal issues consumer services dealt with tended to border on the absurd most of the time. Some people would write in and say they'd contracted a tobacco-related illness and if the company didn't give them a million pounds and buy them a Ferrari, they were going to go to the newspapers.

A few customers complained of finding foreign objects in their cigarettes: pieces of plastic or metal, or human hair. Automatic assembly lines weren't perfect, and mistakes did happen. Sometimes there were nineteen cigarettes in a pack rather than twenty. It happened, but if you smoked, you knew this was rare.

The company wanted to communicate with its customers and make sure they were happy, so they took every complaint and query seriously.

Considering the anti-smoking attitudes gathering strength at the time, the company didn't receive as many negative letters as you might think. Still, any letter that could be perceived as litigious was sent to the lawyer. For example, someone once complained that a cigarette had exploded when it was lit. He thought this was an exaggeration, but after bringing it up with R & D, he discovered it could actually happen. Air pockets!

Some complaints came in about the advertising and, surprisingly, about those health warnings. For eight months, the lawyer corresponded with one customer who was determined to challenge every single health warning on each pack of cigarettes. Talk about customer loyalty.

A lot of people wrote in with little stories, or to say they were searching for tobacco-related memorabilia—old posters and hats, that sort of thing.

Of course, because the consumer services department was the mouthpiece of the company, for legal reasons the department needed to be careful in all of its responses. He was always respectful that people had taken the time to get in touch. In an industry that was losing consumers by the day, the company wanted to ensure that its customers felt cared for.

There was nastiness occasionally: death threats. Those were isolated incidents and were reported to the police, as they would be at any company.

People also wrote in claiming the taste of the cigarettes had changed and wanting to know why, which reminded him of R & D's impossible challenge of changing the recipe without changing the flavour. The most common answer, though, was that the customer had purchased an old batch. Though cigarettes didn't have a best-before date on the packet, they did have a shelf life of somewhere between six and eighteen months.

Perhaps the most surprising thing was the rising number of customers complaining about the poor taste and quality of the products. The team sent packs of returned cigarettes to R & D for testing. This was how he began to learn about the growth of the counterfeit market. As tobacco products became more expensive, more counterfeit versions were entering the country—from China, for example. These contained poor quality tobacco, with tar and nicotine levels that were off the charts. Smokers bought them because they were often a lot less expensive—up to 75 percent cheaper. In his opinion, they probably should have known better. No such thing as a free lunch, right?

He watched R & D test some of these counterfeit products. What was amazing was how they stank, though they were still tobacco. The nightmare scenario would have been a poisoned counterfeit product killing a customer. But he never came across that kind of case in his time at the company.

One afternoon, he received a frantic call from one of the consumer services executives who dealt with the phone line for customers. She sounded shaken.

Usually, when team members wanted legal advice, they filled out a form and sent it to him. This circumstance was clearly different. The executive told him that a consumer representative had mistakenly given the lawyer's full name to a customer who had just called.

The caller, an older woman, had insisted on talking to one of the company lawyers, and the consumer rep had promised to make sure she got through to the legal department and had given her the lawyer's number. But revealing his name was against company pro-tocol. For example, whenever he sent letters out to people, he never signed his name; they were always signed "Legal Department."

The woman who called had a name too: Mrs. Brown. And she did call him.

Later that day, he was sitting, smoking, in his office with that beautiful view of the valley when his phone rang. He picked up.

"Is this Mr. _____?" a woman said.

"Yes."

"Are you the company lawyer?"

He was a lawyer with the company, he answered.

Then she said this to him: "I just want you to know that the love of my life, my husband, who I've been married to for over fifty years, died yesterday of lung cancer."

He didn't know what to say.

She continued: "He was a lifelong smoker and supporter of your brand, which he smoked up to the day of his death. Even in illness, he was unable to quit."

He still didn't know what to say.

"I've lost the love of my life," she told him. "I don't want any money, and I don't want any sympathy. I'm not going to sue you. I just want you people to know that you've ruined my life."

And then she hung up the phone.

He sat there for what seemed like hours. For the first time since joining the company, he was overwhelmed with doubt—in him-self, and in what he was doing. He thought about quitting, and that prospect floated uncomfortably in the stillness of his spacious new office.

It was a moment of choice, and after thinking it through, he made one.

He was a lawyer working in an industry that was 100 percent legal. He was supporting his wife and building a foundation for their family and their shared future. He'd made a vow to his wife, and now he made a vow to himself: he wouldn't look back. He would do everything in his power to succeed in his new role. He was not going to let this bereaved woman, or anyone for that matter, get in the way.

Over the next ten years, he visited dozens of countries—every country in Europe, including a few that some North Americans have never heard of: San Marino, Andorra, Liechtenstein. Most tourists went to the Vatican to be blessed by the Pope, but did they know they could also buy a carton of duty-free Marlboros on the way out? Marlboro manufactured a special package exclusively for sale in Vatican City.

He travelled to Russia, Kurdistan, Mongolia, Azerbaijan, Uzbekistan, and Kazakhstan. These were mostly growth markets. Mongolia, by the way, then had one of the highest smoking rates in the world, at 47 percent. He visited Japan, Malaysia, Singapore, Puerto Rico, the Dominican Republic, Mexico, Brazil, Morocco, Egypt, Algeria, South Africa, Nigeria, and China, home to three hundred million of the world's one billion smokers. Another ninety-four million lived in India, which he never was able to visit on company business.

Not one jurisdiction in all the countries he visited had the same regulations when it came to selling tobacco, which is exactly why he was so busy.

His favourite jurisdiction was Spain.

FAKE SPAIN

In his next life, he will be Spanish. He will smoke in the warm sunshine all year long, and he will eat dinner after nine every night.

Spain was the first international market for which the company gave him legal responsibility—the next step in his education.

Inductions were over, and he'd passed; he'd learned the basics about manufacturing, retail, marketing, consumer services, and he'd taken a lead role at the company in the implementation of the new EU directives, including restrictions on tobacco advertising. Now, less than a year after starting with the company, Mary was giving him a geographical arena to patrol, and a market to manage: the Iberia file.

The file spanned the Iberian Peninsula—Spain, Portugal, Andorra, Gibraltar—and the Canary Islands. His job was to ensure that all of the company's marketing and advertising campaigns adhered to the laws of each land. The hub of the Iberia file was in Madrid.

On the lawyer's first visit there, he was told the following story, on numerous occasions, by many different people. Here's the shortest version: Rodrigo de Jerez was one of the Spanish crewmen who sailed on Christopher Columbus's first voyage across the Atlantic, in 1492. He brought back with him a pleasurable pastime acquired from the Indigenous inhabitants of what we now call the Bahamas: smoking tobacco. It is Jerez who is often identified as being European smoker number one, the sailor who travelled across the sea and brought back with him a golden vice. And that vice had swept across Europe.

Why did so many people in Madrid tell him this story? Were they proud of it?

The lawyer wasn't sure. It did seem that Spain was ground zero for European smokers. And now, more than five hundred years later, while most of Europe was doing its best to stamp the vice out, Spain was looking like the last bastion for Western Europe's smokers. It was still a smoker's paradise, where approximately 40 percent of Jerez's compatriots still smoked.

The lawyer couldn't think of anything better than travelling to Madrid on business. And lucky for him, he ended up jetting there at least 150 times over the next ten years.

In many ways, Madrid was the opposite of London. If London was shades of grey, distant, and chilly, Madrid was full-colour, vivacious, and hot. Faces here were tanned, relaxed, and the food was exceptional—not sausage and potatoes but rare beef and paella. Spain was a seductive smile after a bottle of wine, and the attitude here was summed up poetically in one word: *mañana*, "tomorrow" —it didn't all have to get done that day.

In London, he often sported dark pants and blazers, but in celebration of his new file, he bought a couple of suits especially for his Madrid visits, which his wife affectionately referred to as his "man from Del Monte suits." He still has them hanging in his closet, though they no longer fit. You know the suit: light beige, an "American abroad, could be a spy" suit. Neutral, and yet somehow mysterious.

An agenda was prepared, and he was dispatched south.

On his early morning flight from London to Madrid, the captain and co-pilot were smoking in the cockpit; he could smell the cigarette smoke from business class.

He asked the attendant if smoking was allowed on the flight. She said there was no smoking. He pointed out he could smell cigarette smoke, but she pretended not to understand him. In the wake of 9/11, travel etiquette had changed, but it seemed that pilots could still smoke in their locked cockpit.

The terminal in Madrid was also filled with smoke. And when he entered the company's office, in downtown Madrid, it could not have been smokier. Everyone was puffing away. It felt like another era. There might as well have been typewriters and bottles of tequila on the desks.

In some ways, the company had given him one of the easiest markets to manage his first time out. In late 2001, Spain was by far the friendliest environment in Europe towards tobacco advertising and promotion, and his colleagues in Madrid turned out to be quite possibly the most cheerful, as well as most stylish, people he had ever worked with. They were as cool, or cooler, than Leah.

No wonder they were jovial: the tobacco industry in Spain enjoyed freedoms that didn't exist anywhere else in the West. With the exception of television advertising, pretty much all other marketing was legal, including all forms of print and billboard advertising, giveaways, and promotions. This was a far cry from other shrinking markets across Europe, where many of these freedoms had vanished years earlier, and were continuing to disappear.

Marketing freedom meant that the lawyer could approve innovative and creative ad campaigns. He could actually say "yes" here. This, of course, helped him get along with his new colleagues.

His first day ended like this. He was working with the senior team when, at 9:30 P.M., one of them, Fernando, asked him, "Do you drink?"

"Yes," he answered.

Fernando went to the office fridge, handed him a beer, and the others joined him.

A few beers in, they decided to go for dinner, to a place called Casa Matias, a Basque restaurant, where they ate some of the most incredible beef he'd had in his life.

They finished dinner at 12:30 A.M. He was loaded; he actually couldn't see straight. All he knew was he had to get some sleep before getting up for more meetings the next day. A couple of his new co-workers took him back to his hotel, and he passed out in his man from Del Monte suit.

The next morning was foggy. He had breakfast in the hotel and was horrified to see so many people smoking and drinking alcohol at breakfast. He had a few cigarettes, a cup of coffee, and nothing to eat.

When he showed up to the office, he was greeted differently.

Fernando shook his hand, and the women kissed him good morning on his cheek. This was the life.

He spent an hour in the meeting room and then took a cab to meet with an external law firm that assisted with local legal advice.

The lawyers there invited him to lunch in a partners' dining room with a spectacular view of Madrid. Once again, the meal clock was different here; almost no one ate lunch before 2 P.M. Copious amounts of booze were consumed, and the lunch extended until 4 P.M. Following lunch, he made a mad dash for the airport to catch an evening flight back to London. He staggered onto the plane and slumped into his seat, pretending to scan international headlines from his *Herald Tribune* newspaper.

He felt guilty about not being able to work on the flight home because of the booze he'd consumed. Thankfully, he worked for a British company and no one ever questioned any of his alcohol expenses. So he put his seat back, enjoyed a gin and tonic—or two—and prepared himself for the looks of disapproval, and maybe a hint of jealousy, from his wife for arriving home drunk and happy.

Spain was a strategically important market for his company, and for reasons you might not expect.

In all of these settings—the office, the meetings, long lunches, late dinners, and after-work drinks—everyone smoked, all the time. Mostly, they smoked Spain's national brand of cigarettes: Fortuna. And that was just fine.

His company's interest in Spain had virtually nothing to do with the smoking culture of the Spanish. His professional mission there was partly to study how people in Northern Europe—mostly British and Irish—behaved when they went on vacation.

He took much pleasure from learning about the real Spain, but plenty of people from the UK came here to see a fake version of the county—the fun-house-mirror version of a vacation experience, which was designed by travel and hospitality, booze, and tobacco companies. This market for their products was booming because of British and Irish tourists, who flocked to Spain for weekend get-aways, sun, fun, and sex—possibly not with their spouses—and a lot of drinking and smoking. That's why he was sent there: to make sure that when UK tourists smoked on vacation, they smoked his company's brands.

He did not like Fake Spain, although he came to know it well.

In England, when the upper middle classes went on vacation, they jetted to Tuscany or Provence, rented houses in the countryside, in vineyards, or on the ocean, ate roasted red peppers and fine cuts of meat, and washed those meals down with a superb and complex wine.

The working and middle classes often went to Fake Spain, where a one-week vacation including meals and return airfare could cost as little as £199. As they said in Britain, it was "as cheap as chips." People who lived on government benefits went on holiday too, and they often chose Fake Spain. The drive teams he'd met in those early weeks had probably all been to Fake Spain. The employees at the factory in Belfast came to Fake Spain.

Because in Fake Spain, unlike Real England, there was sunshine, blue sky, and beaches of soft sand—not those big pebbles in Brighton that you needed shoes to walk on, and could not, let's be honest, recline on with comfort.

There were two hot spots for Fake Spain vacations: Costa del Sol and Ibiza. They were only slightly different in their DNA.

Ibiza was a world-famous destination for partying, all night dancing, drugs, going to bed at dawn. It was more for the under-twenty-five set. Málaga, on the Costa del Sol, was marginally less testosterone charged, and only slightly less tacky. It was for tourists in their late twenties and older in search of vitamin-D-enhanced alcohol.

On one of his first visits to Spain, his agenda was to go on a market tour to Málaga, watch the people on vacation, see how they behaved, and learn about all of the marketing forces wrapped around their vacation experience.

The lawyer's first reactions to Fake Spain: he couldn't believe the number of British, Irish, and German bars and restaurants crammed into one little fake town. He couldn't believe that a person could spend an entire week in Spain and not speak a single word of Spanish, or that pints—even pitchers—of beer could be priced as low as one euro. He couldn't believe that a person could visit a foreign country and sample none of the local food, or that there were entire hotels filled with young men and women who were allowed to behave outrageously at any given hour of the day or night without being arrested by the Spanish authorities. And from a marketing perspective, he couldn't believe that tobacco companies were giving away bottles of booze with a carton of cigarettes. Big bottles of vodka and Scotch—free!

What he saw when he toured Fake Spain was a party that lasted all day and all night, where people drank, and drank, and drank, and smoked, and smoked, and smoked. To put it in perspective, because of Spain's tax rates, for the price of one pack of cigarettes in the UK, you could almost buy a carton of them in Fake Spain.

He stayed for a night to watch how the vacation experience unfolded and felt like a disapproving parent. It was not like he was born yesterday; he'd spent a few years trolling London nightclubs. But this was different. It was like a frat party he thought he'd never have to go back to—except instead of college kids, it was fully grown adults. Drunkenness surprised him at every turn. It was embarrassing to watch, but it also happened to be the perfect forum to sell an unholy numbers of cigarettes.

In Málaga, here's a breakdown of how a basic day unfolded.

The typical tourist would wake up in the morning, not early, but before 10 A.M. Their English breakfast was paid for: baked beans, fried potatoes, sausages, bacon, toast, tea or coffee. It was probably a buffet, and it was feeding time for people stocking up for the day. He noticed some tourists making sandwiches and stuffing them in their bags for later on.

After breakfast, there was the usual rush for chairs at the pool, or at the beach. Regrettably, the Germans had probably already been down there, hours before, and reserved those chairs with towels. That's why his company started giving away Union Jack towels, to compete with the Germans. Excellent promotional material, those towels, in his opinion.

Whether you were British or German, though, the drinking usually started at about 11 A.M. And it continued well into the afternoon. Drinking by the ocean, drinking before a dip in the pool, drinking after a swim in the full sun of mid-afternoon. This was the time of day when Spaniards were having lunch and a siesta, making sure to stay in the shade. Tourists were there to get tanned, to fry in the Andalusian sun, and to drink while they did so. So slather on that sunscreen, crack open a beer, and bake. This went on all afternoon.

It wasn't until about 4 or 5 P.M. that the tourists retreated to their hotel rooms, because they'd had too much to drink, or too much sun, or both. They headed back up to the protection of their hotels: for sex, for rest, for games of pool or foosball.

A few hours later they emerged, reenergized in party clothes. The women wearing very short skirts, too much makeup, and jewellery. The men in tight jeans and T-shirts, slick-gelled hair, and cologne.

Then they headed into "town."

Being in town, in Málaga, meant they walked through the streets to a restaurant for dinner. But, of course, they dined in tourist restaurants, with tourist menus, all in English. The food was not remotely related to the food he was enjoying in Madrid. Food here was cheap in price and low in quality. Alcohol the same. No one seemed to care. No one was here for the food. It was just like London, or Bristol, or Manchester late at night, only it was warm out, and maybe the streets had a few cobblestones and some cute old-style European street lamps.

After dinner, everyone gravitated to a bar, English-style pub, or nightclub to party. All of these options served cheap drinks. There were pickup joints if you were younger, or pubs if you just wanted to sit and survey, sip and smoke.

And then it was a question of how long you could last. Were you a three-, four-, or five-drink kind of personality? How many drinks, exactly, would it take before you could not function properly, before the person at the end of the bar started to look attractive, or before you forgot about the challenges you were having at work or with your family?

After about 11 P.M., police started roaming the town to help with the drunks.

If you were a hard-core drinker, then you were in the crowd heading out of the clubs for late-night bites to help cut the booze. This was when there was a lot of stumbling through the streets looking kind of sad and confused.

He recalled seeing a hammered young woman in her twenties stop walking in the middle of the road, lying down, and passing out with her skirt above her hips. Surprise: no underwear! Another image: a loaded and sad-looking lad flirting with a woman whose leg was wounded and bleeding. Was that sexy?

The lads were roving in packs, ogling women, singing, shouting, and maybe even getting into a good old-fashioned brawl à la *Fight Club*. On that trip, as he strolled down one of those streets, a woman teetered up to him. She looked at him through cloudy eyes and then loudly asked this opening question: "Hey, you wanna fuck?"

Late at night in Málaga: it was like watching the collapse of Western civilization.

From a strategic perspective, he learned there were specific times during the vacation cycle in which the company wanted to entice these clients to buy their product. The package tours usually ran from Thursday to Thursday, or Sunday to Sunday. So you tried to get vacationers that first night, when they were giddy and had money in their pockets. Specifically, you wanted to get them in that sweet spot right after dinner, before the evening drinking marathon, before they were making "distressed purchases" from the bartender.

The retailers in town were roping them in, and they were not like any stores in the UK.

Here, in Fake Spain, the government had allowed retailers to build consumer cathedrals to tobacco and alcohol. These superstores sold phone cards, magazines, postcards, lighters, and booze, but their focus was selling tobacco—cartons of tobacco. You walked into a store and there were aisles and aisles of cigarette cartons from floor to ceiling: a mini version of the factory warehouse in Northern Ireland.

A tourist could buy four cartons of cigarettes at a time, enticed by a free bottle of vodka—but only if they bought four cartons. Give them something of value that would incentivize them to buy more, and they would. An important consideration was the very low tax on alcohol as well. This was a bizarre tourist world where bottled water could cost as much or more than a beer.

Why was a UK company putting all of this effort into these tourist markets?

The answer was simple. They did it because the competition was here, and if his company didn't play in this arena, their competitors would dominate it. The tourists would associate their new vacation brand with their fun memories of the trip and buy that brand when they were back in depressing, grey, nine-to-five London.

Bottles of booze, beach towels, and T-shirts became weapons in this marketing war. It was what the drive teams did, but in the middle of a raging party: a showcase for their brands that simply didn't exist on home turf.

The vacation markets were one of the last and best ways to advertise their product legally to UK citizens, in a staging area outside of the UK.

Giveaways, for example, used to be legal as a marketing tool in the UK, but no longer. And it was an area that he could immediately see improving on in Fake Spain.

The team here gave away different products every week, but why not use the same giveaways all year long? After all, this was a once-a-year cycle. It wasn't as if the same people were coming back week after week. Free branded T-shirts—all year. And if it turned into a wet T-shirt contest? Well, that was crossing the line. But, hey, this was a party culture, and cigarettes were an important feature of the party.

Basically, it was a captive audience—and every campaign in Spain was 100 percent legal.

There was one more reason why tourists bought UK cigarette brands by the carton in Spain. The European Union's free movement of goods made it perfectly legal for British and Irish tourists to purchase as much tobacco in Spain as they could carry and bring it home, as long as it was for personal consumption. At the time, a pack of cigarettes in Spain was at least two-thirds cheaper than the average pack in the UK.

It didn't take a genius to work out whether these tourists were buying cigarettes for their friends or for themselves. If you filled your suitcase with cheap tobacco, you could save a lot of money for yourself, or make a profit by selling packs to your friends. It was not uncommon for smokers to bring back a year's worth of cigarettes to the UK. Nor was it uncommon for smokers to get on airplanes, fly down to Málaga for the day, have a nice Spanish lunch, and fill up their bags with sticks.

The savings were enormous; they could be in the thousands of pounds. And who was to say it *wasn't* for personal use? It wasn't as if a customs agent was going to come to your house to check that you alone were smoking all of those cigarettes.

In Fake Spain, his tobacco company remained a leading UK brand. The never-ending party was his company's sweet spot, for now.

But the battleground was shifting in terms of marketing and advertising restrictions for tobacco. During the lawyer's time managing the Iberia file, the country that introduced tobacco to Europe was transitioning from being a relatively free market for advertising tobacco to becoming a more familiar Western European market.

Doors were closing, thanks to those European Union directives he'd spent so much time on in the UK. They were being implemented in Spain as well; it just took a little longer here. *Mañana.*

Once you left the party and returned to Madrid, it got a little lonely out there for his company's brands. In fact, the concept of a British-based company selling sticks in Spain was a relatively new one.

Spain's rulers had for hundreds of years tightly controlled all aspects of the tobacco industry, which over the centuries had delivered a constantly flowing stream of wealth to generations of the royal family, the dictator who deposed them, and most recently to the democratic monarchy of Spain.

Legend had it that when Rodrigo de Jerez returned home from his New World voyage and his neighbours witnessed the sailor using tobacco, they freaked out; after all, smoke was pouring out of his mouth. Jerez had obviously been possessed by the devil, it was decided, and so he was promptly imprisoned—for many years, apparently.

It must have been quite surreal for Jerez, upon his release, to see that tobacco was in demand. It was shortly thereafter that the French ambassador in Spain—Jean Nicot, after whom nicotine was named —imported the addictive substance to the court of Catherine de' Medici, Queen of France: the rest is history.

Meanwhile, Spain rapidly evolved into the most powerful empire in existence as its conquistadors seized America's resources. It didn't take long for its monarchy to claim ownership of the tobacco trade. Starting in 1636, if a citizen anywhere in the Spanish empire bought tobacco, it was courtesy of the king and queen, who reaped massive profits from every part of the supply chain, from farming in far-off colonies—in lands we now call Colombia, Cuba, Mexico, Peru, the Philippines, and Venezuela—to manufacturing and sales both at home and abroad.

Centuries later, had things changed?

Well, the empire had collapsed. But what the lawyer saw in Spain was that throughout the mainland, cigarettes could still only be sold at specific stores, which everyone simply called *estancos*. These were like newsstands, selling smokes, phone cards, magazines, and bubble gum—fast-moving consumer goods. This network of state tobacconists had been set up to sell cigarettes efficiently on a per capita basis of one *estanco* for every fifteen thousand citizens. The lawyer learned that the word *estanco* could be translated either as "tobacco store" or "state monopoly," because in Spain the act of selling tobacco and the concept of a state monopoly had become indistinguishable.

To this day in Spain, the price of a pack of cigarettes was approved by the government, so all players involved knew their expected shares of tobacco profits: those margins were fixed.

Meanwhile, over hundreds of years, the all-powerful crown tobacco corporation had morphed into the more friendly sounding Tabacalera company, which continued to control the distribution of all tobacco products to all *estancos* in the Spanish mainland. Basically, Tabacalera had maintained the spirit of its national monopoly. Then, in 1999, Tabacalera had merged with France's centuries-old, state-owned tobacco monopoly to become a super-sized regional player called Altadis, all in an effort to stave off being acquired by a larger, richer, and ever-hungry American or British tobacco company.

At street level, owning an *estanco* really did seem to the lawyer like having a licence to print money, since the shops were selling cigarettes to a given population of smokers within a sector of fifteen thousand neighbours. In most regions of Spain, because of the per capita design of the system, there was almost no competition between the stores.

This meant it was up to the tobacco company's sales reps in their smoky Madrid office to convince the *estanco* owners, who in turn had to convince the singular, just-shy-of-a-monopoly national distributor, that their foreign brand was a product the owners should have on the shelf competing with Spanish cigarettes. Good luck to them! And there were no drive teams here. There was no point; that concept couldn't function in a monopoly.

In a tourist area like southern Spain, no problem. Anywhere else in Spain, the basic attitude was *vete a la mierda*, "go fuck yourself." No one was interested in selling their British sticks—except in Fake Spain, that is, where they'd built those alcohol and cigarette cathedrals, which were, in reality, technically considered *estancos*.

If there was a silver lining to this antiquated, near-monopolized system, it could be summed up in one word: data.

Only because of the efficiency of the *estanco* set-up, his sales group were able to trace every pack they sold across Spain. They knew exactly where their business hot spots were, and other than the tourist traps, there weren't a lot of them.

That's why it was strange when someone on the Madrid staff spied a startling anomaly. According to said data, one *estanco* was selling a disproportionately large amount of their company's product countrywide.

It didn't make any sense. So they double- and triple-checked the numbers. The data seemed correct, and it stubbornly showed that a massive volume of their company's brands were being sold from just a single *estanco*. It wasn't even a store in the middle of Madrid or Barcelona. It was far away in the north, near the border with France—and far, far away from Fake Spain.

The lawyer figured it was worth a field trip.

So, the man from Del Monte arranged a meeting with the owner of this *estanco* in the tiny northern town.

It was a lovely train ride through the Spanish countryside, and when he pulled into the charming border town, the owner greeted him warmly at his *estanco*. The man was probably in his fifties, had a well-groomed moustache, was dressed in business casual, and had on a very nice pair of shoes that were possibly the shiniest, most well-polished shoes the lawyer had ever seen.

He looked sharp, and his *estanco* was nice and clean, but there appeared to be absolutely nothing extraordinary about it.

The man with gleaming shoes invited the lawyer for coffee, and they strolled to a café near his *estanco*. He was quite popular, it seemed. Everyone they passed nodded or smiled at him in recognition. It sort of felt like he was walking down Main Street with the sheriff or the mayor.

The lawyer learned that the man with gleaming shoes owned the café too. It also turned out he owned the hotel across the street, as well as numerous other businesses in town. He had amassed a small empire here, in this border town—all of which, he proudly explained to the lawyer, he'd purchased in the last few years from the profits from his *estanco*.

This was slightly confusing. How did the owner of a single *estanco* in a small town suddenly have the means to buy up so much around him? After all, in theory, all *estanco* owners should roughly make the same amount of money, because each was selling to a population of about the same size.

It's not like every *estanco* owner across Spain had suddenly had three banner years. The rates of smoking were relatively stable in all regional areas, with the exception of Fake Spain, where the thriving European tourist market pushed rising sales, a factor that wasn't taken into account when dividing up geographical areas and gifting licences.

The man with gleaming shoes smoked Fortuna, the favoured Spanish national brand. He spoke some English, but they transitioned into French—a language they both spoke. They sat down with coffees and smoked while the man explained, *en français,* the amazing tobacco anomaly he was profiting from.

He was profiting so strongly, he openly admitted, because he had been selling a massive amount of cigarettes to French citizens, right across the border.

Why would the French come to Spain to buy their cigarettes?

Easy: a few years earlier, the French government had increased tobacco duties to a significantly higher rate than in Spain. Remember that banderol in the Northern Irish factory, the stamp that represented a tax value? In France, the government had imposed higher tobacco duties in the hopes of reducing its rate of smoking, putting the cost of a pack of cigarettes at about five euros. In Spain, the same pack cost less than two euros—a massive price differential.

The border between France and Spain was nothing—not like crossing from San Diego to Tijuana. Instead, there was a sign that said you were entering France or Spain. Border controls had been removed many years ago under the Schengen Agreement.

The Schengen Agreement (which didn't include the UK and Ireland) meant that immigrants entering into Southern Europe— along with any European residents—were able to travel unrestricted all the way from Greece to the northern-most parts of Germany and France. A French citizen could simply drive, bike, or even walk into Spain and not have to chat with a single border guard.

This man's fortune was built on the Schengen Agreement, French government tax hikes on tobacco, and geographical good luck.

More specifically, it was built on the French government's policy in response to the global assault on tobacco.

Business for the man with gleaming shoes now extended past his set Spanish customer base to the thousands of French smokers who were able to visit—at the drop of a hat—his totally average store. They could even converse with him in their local language, as he spoke French. They could purchase as many cigarettes as they wished and simply bring them home. All completely legal.

Over coffee, the man described the threats he'd received from French tobacco sellers across the border. They were outraged that he was stealing their customers and, they figured, their money. He'd beefed up security as a result. Just to put this in context: this one man was selling millions of dollars' worth of cigarettes a year because of his unique situation.

Indeed, the man with gleaming shoes seemed very happy. After all, he was buying up his entire town. Coffee was on the house, he informed the lawyer.

Mystery solved.

The lawyer returned to Madrid a satisfied detective.

Higher taxes on sticks had made this one man a fortune, but he wasn't the only one benefiting when governments raised taxes on cigarettes. The term *blowback*, coined by the CIA in the 1950s, meant the unintended results of a political action. Blowback was definitely the right word to use in describing how government tax hikes had fuelled the counterfeit market in cigarettes. And perhaps there was no better place to see that result on display than in Gibraltar.

PIRATE TOWN

His mother always told him that if he had nothing good to say about a suspicious city-state overrun by tourists, sailors, crime, and pirates, then don't say anything at all.

When he started looking after Spain, he also had to manage Gibraltar.

Gibraltar was not dissimilar to many city-states with no taxes, in that more tobacco products were sold here for every man, woman, and child than could ever possibly be consumed by them.

Translation: Gibraltar was a notorious port for smuggling illegal cigarettes into mainland Europe, where profit margins were high and penalties low.

Ever battled your way through the tourists, pickpockets, and general chaos of London's Trafalgar Square, perhaps wondering why that massive Corinthian column guarded silently by four bronze lions looms over the perpetual snarling traffic? It's all to commemorate a military victory, of course: when the Royal Navy defeated the combined might of the French and Spanish fleets.

This was way back in 1805, during the Napoleonic Wars. That epic clash of colonial titans took place on the waves near Cape Trafalgar, and halted Napoleon's plan to invade England. It all happened just around the bend from Gibraltar—a highly valued, strategic naval outpost located on the southernmost edge of the Iberian Peninsula, which Britain had officially taken possession of in 1713. This slice of hot, dry land guarded a precious waterway—the Straight of Gibraltar—for any ships hoping to cross between the Mediterranean and the Atlantic; Britain's safe harbour on this sliver of sunny real estate helped maintain its naval supremacy into the early twentieth century.

Gibraltar, therefore, remained a diplomatic annoyance to the Spanish authorities, who were ever responsible for patrolling the border of this tiny British enclave rudely located on the very tip of this otherwise Spanish cape. It was an afterthought for the British authorities who controlled it, reminiscent of colonial times: a world where a flag flew in a far-flung corner of an empire, though no one in power seemed to pay much attention to what actually went on there, unless something went horribly wrong.

In that sense, the Brits did an excellent job of maintaining Gibraltar as an outpost for their navy, but they did a lousy job when it came to monitoring counterfeit cigarette operations. The lawyer came to see Gibraltar as a giant sieve, where counterfeit sticks flowed from Africa and Asia into Europe.

His company, like all tobacco companies, sold legitimate tobacco products into Gibraltar. Those products were made in the factory in Northern Ireland and transported here. They were sold in Gibraltar largely because it was a duty-free zone that was popular with tourists passing through on cruise ships, and popular with the military passing through on warships. And they sold to the old British fishermen who still lived here, looking as if they'd come to life from a sepia-toned imperial postcard.

They also sold to those people who were interested in crossing over from southern Spain for the day, probably making the journey specifically to take advantage of the lower price point in Gibraltar on items such as cigarettes, booze, or whatever else they were searching for. Goods in general were cheaper here.

The border between Spain and Gibraltar was not like Spain's border with France. The Schengen Agreement, remember, had not been signed by the UK. This border was more like East and West Berlin back in Cold War era, despite the fact that Spain and the UK were at peace with each other and at the time were both acting members in the EU.

But beware! If you were crossing that border, the Spanish authorities, knowing that Gibraltar had become a pirate town, felt the need to inspect every person, package, and car entering and exiting the enclave. The border guards made a show of it—a sassy statement—slowing down traffic in and out to put pressure on the British authorities to hand this contested piece of ground back to Spain, which the British were probably never going to do. Basically, the lawyer figured, the Spanish were pissed off that Britain still retained control of Gibraltar, and their self-righteous attitude was on full display at the border. In this sense, the border security was more like a piece of avant-garde political theatre.

It was that sore-loser attitude that made it impossible to fly directly from Spain to Gibraltar. If you were coming from Spain, you had to drive. But the lines at the border were so damn long, you were better off parking your car, walking across as a pedestrian, and getting a taxi to take you into ye olde town centre.

And, wow, this cobblestoned town really felt like bygone Britain. There were old-fashioned letter boxes, red telephone boxes, crooked-walled pubs, and row upon row of stores selling British cigarettes and other duty-free UK products.

The lawyer was surprised to see how much of the population was of British descent, running the hotels, restaurants, and pubs, and servicing the British military base. It was a surreal place, out of a John le Carré novel. He could sense criminal activity in the breeze, but without ever actually seeing it.

The lawyer's work in Gibraltar wasn't *really* about making sure their product was here; it was on the shelves and behind counters. Instead, he was dealing with constant issues arising from counterfeit or questionable products, dodgy packs of cigarettes that would eventually wind up at the consumer services desk at HQ, where they were often passed on to R & D for analysis.

To help the lawyer trawl for evidence of black-market products slipping into the Gibraltar port, he worked with a local law firm, and they did their piece to monitor the illicit trade. In practical terms, it meant working with the police to obtain search-and-seizure orders for suspect warehouses or any other kind of legal injunction —all to protect the company's rights, its products, and its reputation against the booming counterfeit industry. But it didn't take the lawyer long to realize this was a losing battle.

It was a losing battle because Gibraltar was a small place, and it was impossible to keep a secret there—even in closed court. By the time their team showed up with a search-and-seizure order at a storage facility or shop, everything was already gone. He never figured out if the leaks were in the court system, among the police, or within his own legal firm. Or coming from all three, for that matter.

Rule: in Gibraltar, the bad guys always won.

That's why this was a pirate town. To be clear, Monaco was a pirate town as well, but Monaco had wealthy-looking pirates, sophisticated-looking pirates, pirates in well-tailored suits who drove Ferraris.

Not so in Gibraltar, where the style was more low-key. You couldn't tell who the pirates were in Gibraltar.

His local connection was a man named Juan. Once, early on, while Juan was giving him a market tour, they walked into a store and Juan instructed the lawyer, "Ask them in English if they have any grey-market products that are not on display."

The lawyer looked around the store. This place had a lot of cigarettes, thousands of cartons stacked high to the ceiling. They only sold cartons of cigarettes and liquor, rack after rack of sticks and booze. And it was all duty-free. Or at least they called themselves duty-free, but a person didn't need a boarding pass to shop here. Gibraltar, in a way, was sort of like the world's largest duty-free store, and it sat at the edge of the ocean: a store for all the pirates cruising the waves between Africa and Europe.

The lawyer followed Juan's orders and asked the sales clerk if they could take a look at anything that wasn't on the shelf—a secret stash kind of thing.

The man didn't even hesitate. He even seemed eager to go into the back and bring out a carton for them. Low and behold, it was their company's brand of cigarettes.

The sales clerk handed the lawyer the carton, which he inspected closely. The shrink wrap wasn't as tight on the carton as it would be if it were manufactured in their Northern Irish factory. And the printing on the packaging looked a little off-kilter, but he might not have known the difference if it wasn't his job to know.

The cigarettes could either have been made legitimately by an African-based licensed factory or in one of the hundreds of counterfeit factories that had sprung up to take advantage of the high taxes consumers were now paying on each pack in various parts of the world.

The lawyer was never told where those counterfeit factories were, or how many, specifically, existed. Before this job, he'd heard a lot about counterfeit designer bags and watches, but not cigarettes.

Juan purchased the carton from the shopkeeper.

They took it outside and opened it. In it they found eight packs. Usually, a carton had ten.

They opened one of the packs and took out a cigarette. It was obvious it wasn't professionally made in a high-tech factory. The lawyer put it under his nose and took a whiff. The cigarette sort of smelled like piss, he thought.

Juan watched as the lawyer put it in his mouth, lit it up, and inhaled. The smoke smelled different—the flavour wasn't right— but while it definitely wasn't smooth, it wasn't unsmokable.

They'd have to send this to the R & D team in Northern Ireland. They had the skills and tech to rip it apart, analyze it—and then file it away in storage with the rest of their incredible collection of global cigarettes.

With advertising restrictions and tax hikes, counterfeit cigarette sales were on the rise internationally. Gibraltar was just a small piece of a much larger and complex web—a web that seemed almost invisible, even as you got tangled in it.

Billions of cigarettes were sold each year on the black market, according to reports. They came from illegal factories and operations all over the planet. Some high tech, some low. They were popping up in Malaysia, in the Philippines, in Spain, in France, in South Africa, and increasingly in China, where, apparently, sophisticated factories churned out sticks as efficiently as his company's factories. Rumour had it that some of the Chinese counterfeit facilities were hidden in rural areas under lakes or in caves. He didn't want to know.

Perhaps not that surprisingly, one of the first terrorist organizations to be linked to the counterfeit cigarette industry was the Irish

Republican Army. This may have had something do to with the fact that in Northern Ireland the IRA had one of the largest cigarette manufacturers in the UK right in their backyard: his company.

Regardless of where they were being made, black-market cigarettes were thought by some to be up there with heroin in terms of the trade's size, reach, and profit margins: billions of sticks that were being smoked but were not being taxed. Estimations put the cost of losses to governments at over £50 billion a year.

And ever since the IRA had taken the lead, other terrorist organizations had followed suit. It wasn't difficult to find news articles linking any given terrorist organization or organized crime syndicate—from al Quaeda to the "good" old American Mafia—to the trade in counterfeit cigarettes. It was an excellent way to fill coffers and brought less harsh punishment than if they were caught, say, smuggling heroin.

This was a relatively new phenomenon, though, because the black market seemed to grow in tandem with rising government tax rates on the product. It was blowback from the assault on the tobacco industry.

For the lawyer, the pirate market was a perfect example of Albert Einstein's adage "The more I learn, the more I realize how much I don't know."

The problem was so big, and so mysterious, it was almost abstract. Truth be told, there was only so much the lawyer wanted to know about these dark markets and pirate towns.

One thing was clear to him, though: if he were the prime minister of the UK, he'd hand Gibraltar back to Spain immediately. It wasn't worth the fuss, in his opinion. Let Spain deal with the pirates.

BEACHES OF ASH

The Canary Islands were also part of the Iberia file, and it was his duty to explore all of the regional markets he was responsible for.

He'd never even heard of the Canaries before he was instructed to jet over. And they were not exactly around the corner: it was a four-hour flight from London, southwest, past Spain, past Gibraltar, landing on a dot in the North Atlantic Ocean about one hundred kilometres west of Morocco.

The lawyer was immediately intrigued when he stepped off the plane on his first trip there. He'd come in from a brutally cold winter in London, and on Tenerife, the largest of the seven islands in the Canaries, it was a perfect twenty-five degrees Celsius, the blue sky punctured by the epic shapes of volcanoes rising up on the horizon.

It turned out that the temperature in the Canaries was always thus; in the summer it was on average thirty degrees, in the winter twenty. A loving god seemed to be in control of the thermostat around here.

This sunny cluster of islands was full of contradictions. They were European, although they were nowhere near Europe and were technically floating above the African tectonic plate. They were still controlled by Spain—a souvenir from their colonial empire—although they were distinctly outside of many aspects of the EU. They were isolated, yet people came to the Canaries from all over the world.

The Canaries were popular with British tourists in the wintertime who wanted to remain on European soil but feel they were somewhere exotic. Strategically, this was an important location for the company as a UK tourist market, and because the Canaries were geographically outside of the EU there was no tobacco tax.

This meant that cigarettes were cheap, cheaper than in Fake Spain and cheaper than in Gibraltar. When he first visited, in the early 2000s, a pack of sticks in the UK was about three or four pounds and roughly half that in mainland Spain. Here, on these magnificent islands, it was half that again: one pound a pack.

The Canaries were not only one of the cheapest places to buy cigarettes in "Europe," but one of the cheapest places in the world. It was a smoker's paradise, and the perfect setting for the company to showcase their brands and sell product in high volume to UK tourists, just like in Fake Spain.

The Canaries were kind of like Las Vegas in that the locals welcomed all manner of tourists from different economic brackets and geographies. As a vacation destination, it fit into the cheap holiday category, but there were luxury hotels and attractions here as well. A wealthy European retirement community had sprung up there, and he could see why. It was good for the soul to live in a place like this—and the old souls strolling the beach had a fountain-of-youth vibe to them.

There were other differences too. In mainland Spain, there was the *estanco* business model, which didn't exist here. Instead, tobacco was sold everywhere in the Canaries: in grocery stores, at restaurants and bars, and by people walking around on the beach hawking packs out of beach bags. He could buy cigarettes—legally—while he was stretched out on the sand, and from anyone who wanted to sell him a pack.

Retailers stocked them on shelves with all kinds of other consumer items, because they were so incredibly cheap, and because there were no laws to prevent it.

Cigarettes had gone behind the counter in so many countries not just because of legislation; they had become expensive, valuable enough that stores were targeted for burglaries. Here, though, you could stock them next to canned beans and potato chips. This was something the lawyer had never witnessed in any other jurisdiction.

In the Western world, it was highly unusual to see cigarettes sold with such ease. The sales reps here could literally build pyramids of cigarette cartons on supermarket floors and give away bottles of vodka. A free gift with your purchase was normal in the Canaries.

Why were cigarettes so cheap and easy to buy here in paradise?

The Canaries had a unique manufacturing situation, the lawyer learned.

The government had managed to pull off an economic magic trick by negotiating an extraordinary deal with all major cigarette companies—and by doing so, they had turned the market upside down through a special tax on foreign cigarettes. ·

This foreign tax meant that any cigarettes manufactured outside the Canaries and imported there would be twice or three times as expensive as cigarettes made on sandy home turf.

All those cigarettes created in Northern Ireland with the "Made in the UK" label would be priced out of the market. Ditto with any other brands made off-island. Only cigarettes made by the island's workforce were exempt.

Almost all of the cigarettes smoked in the Canaries were manufactured there by the islanders. Even more improbable, they were
all made in one factory, which was owned by one company: Cita
Tabacos De Canarias, or Cita as everyone called it.

The lawyer was given a tour of the factory.

This was not like the factory in Northern Ireland. It made all the
Spanish brands, all the American brands, and all of the UK brands.
The operation was sleek, streamlined, and high-tech.

The lawyer saw the mighty Marlboro rolling off one line and his
own company's brands of cigarettes rolling off another, all under
one roof. This was not only rare; it was otherwise unheard of, like
visiting a factory that made Coke, Pepsi, and RC Cola, or one that
bottled Budweiser, Coors Light, Heineken, and Canadian.

Cita wasn't just the local player in the islands; it was the only
player.

He'd never seen a set-up like it, and he couldn't understand how
a foreign manufacturer linked to major competitors could have
access to their heavily guarded recipes. It was mind-blowing. Yet
somehow, here in paradise, it didn't seem to matter: *mañana*,
mañana. Whatever the pace was in Madrid, here, it was even slower,
even more relaxed.

The distribution system was different here too.

The grocery stores and corner stores were supplied by one truck
that visited daily—and, yes, it delivered every brand of cigarette.

He noted that when the cigarette truck made the rounds, the
driver would ask each retailer what they wanted to buy. So the stores
would take what they needed each day. It certainly wasn't conven-
tional, but the economy here seemed to have different rules.

It would be like having only one drive team in an entire city and
representing every brand. Again, it was such a relaxed atmosphere
that somehow it all made sense.

The heat, the sky, the waves, and the gentle pace of the day—he fell in love with it all. Initially, he'd visit the Canaries a couple of times a year: for board meetings and marketing conferences. And then his company decided to buy Cita.

The tobacco industry was, and still is, consolidating.

This was because as laws and regulations grew tighter, one sure-fire way to grow a customer base was simply to buy the competition's brands—and therefore their smokers too.

His company was on the acquisition hunt, and this move was an expansion into the Spanish and South American markets. When he'd taken over the Iberia file, his company was a bit player on these islands, and in one fell swoop it became the overseer of the entire tobacco industry in the Canaries.

The acquisition was another step in the lawyer's education.

Back at HQ in London, the lawyer worked with a small team on the Cita deal. For him, it was a steep learning curve. Meanwhile, his elegant and spacious office had become a little more cramped—stacked with cartons and cartons of cigarettes, as well as posters and paraphernalia from various marketing campaigns he was working on. He didn't have enough room anymore for all the cartons of different brands he was promoting; his floor looked like a miniature version of the factory warehouse in Northern Ireland.

The lawyer was also aware he was smoking more, and his wife was aware of it as well.

It made sense. Before he'd joined the company, he'd had to go to a store and pay for the product. Now, it was delivered daily to his desk.

Keep in mind employees received free cigarettes, but for most there was a limit. In his case, though, there was no ceiling; it was a part of his job to study the branding and packaging on multiple brands of sticks.

This meant colleagues sent him carton after carton to examine, and more samples rolled in every week. Every once in a while, he'd have to sort through and throw out a few dozen cartons just to make room for more. Have you ever heard of a smoker throwing out cartons of cigarettes?

And as the lawyer had observed from his earliest days with the company, the negative consequences of all this smoking were never really discussed.

For example: the company was an established UK corporation that stretched back a number of generations, which meant it had a large base of employee alumni. Ex-employees received a regularly published newsletter with updates on what other former employees had accomplished, along with current employee profiles and company news highlights.

The lawyer noted that the newsletter included an obituary section, but those obits never mentioned cancer or any other smoking-related illness as a cause of death. The avoidance of any discussion of smoking's negative impacts was almost absolute. There was no Cancer 101 type of course offered to employees about its hazards. Instead, the emphasis in the company's culture was on corporate responsibility.

His superior, Mary, did not smoke. She was a healthy eater, and a runner. BTW, Mary did not get that promotion, even though she had the near-unanimous support of the entire legal team: he now saw the glass ceiling more clearly.

Sometimes, in meetings, or when Mary dropped by his office and saw how smoky the air was, she would wear an expression of concern. The lawyer could tell his smoking bothered her, and yet she couldn't actually say anything to him about it, because, after all, it was the only product their company made and sold.

———

While he was sorting through the contracts for the Cita deal, he would sometimes smoke a cigarette and find himself fantasizing about visiting those ash-coloured beaches; he could practically feel the warm breeze.

The lawyer wanted to share that Canary experience with his wife —who definitely needed a break from the constant grey and grind of London.

So, when he was informed that an upcoming marketing conference was scheduled to take place on the Canaries, he invited her for the weekend and rented them a room at the palatial Gran Hotel Bahía del Duque.

In one of the many sparkling swimming pools, treading water and chatting, they decided it was time to try for a baby—a decision that had one immediate and challenging consequence.

Though he was now in the business of peddling sticks, the lawyer knew that in addition to studies showing negative impacts for women during pregnancy, tobacco-smoking had been shown to have an effect on male fertility—specifically, the quality of semen. The couple agreed that they wanted to give their child the best chance at being born healthy, of entering the world with all possible advantages.

It wasn't as if they had an argument about it. He accepted the conclusion, and he knew what he had to do: give up smoking for a time.

He picked a date, but in the meantime fired up a stick on the beach and ordered a slice of fresh pineapple. It was so peaceful that he almost felt under a spell, which perhaps explained why no matter how many times he stared up at the looming silhouettes of those volcanoes on the horizon, it never occurred to him that they could blow. He listened to the soft sands quietly shifting in the waves— *mañana, mañana*—so far away from the high speed of big city life.

LOSING AT GRAND PRIX

Grand Prix was a special day for the company.

It was designed to be a "wrap you in cotton wool" experience — if you were lucky enough to be invited. This meant the company was taking care of you from dawn to dusk on the day of the event, anticipating your every need and sparing no cost to make sure those needs were met, and then exceeded.

The lawyer's company could invite only a select group of people to the British Grand Prix, the most elite automobile racing event in the UK. These guests were valued customers: the head buyer for Tesco supermarkets; the finance director of the largest cash and carry; the owners of corporate pub chains like the Firkin and Whatever. Remember all those retail channels of sale — it's those executives who owned and ran those empires, otherwise known as Very Important People.

They were VIPs because they represented businesses that spent seven-digit figures on tobacco, on a weekly basis. A seat at Grand Prix was one way for the company to say thank you.

The rest of the invitees were board members and senior executives from the company. The lawyer was attending, but he wasn't hosting any of the VIP clients—even though he was managing the company's legal file with the British Grand Prix as part of his domestic UK duties. He was attending only because there had been a last-minute cancellation and he'd been invited by the marketing director. Basically, the lawyer was filling an empty seat.

Still, this was his chance to see up close how such a major event fit into the larger ecosystem of the company's marketing strategy.

There was one more group on their guest list: national celebrities.

Not *international* celebrities, but national: UK soap opera stars, the bikini model from Page 3, regional football and rugby players. They were attending to attract media attention, and to help advertise the brand.

These home-grown celebs were present to make the event feel familiar, and even loved. The company asked them to wear—and to be photographed in—branded gear and chat up the guests, to smile brightly, touch a shoulder, lean in with all that branded celebrity affection and raise a glass of champagne while the roar of fast and furious race cars pummelled eardrums and made the ground tremble.

Who was not at Grand Prix? Jill and Joe Smoker were not there. They were watching the event on television, in pubs across the nation, in bars across the world.

Who else was not there? No one from the drive teams, none of the factory workers or the R & D scientists. Their bosses weren't there either, or their bosses' bosses. This was corporate entertaining at its finest, and at its most outrageously expensive. The cost for each guest was many thousands of dollars.

The entire day was tightly choreographed for the VIPs, and here's how it unfolded.

Early that morning, each guest was picked up by limousine at their front door, the driver ringing the bell and opening the limo door. "Good morning, ma'am, sir."

The limousine whisked them to a farmhouse in Northamptonshire, where they were ushered into a barn with tables bearing tablecloths and fine place settings for a very classy morning meal. The VIPs were served a hot breakfast, complete with free cigarettes.

While they enjoyed breakfast in the barn, the guests would hear the whirl of an approaching helicopter. The helicopter hovered and touched down in the field next to the barn. When breakfast was finished, the first group of VIPs stepped up into the chopper, then lifted off, bypassing all the weekend traffic below; traffic was for average customers, the airspace above was for the elite, who were too glamorous to be stuck in gridlock.

The chopper swooped over the grandstands at Silverstone motor racing circuit and landed right in the middle of the racetrack—the most audacious entrance possible. Each guest then exited the chopper onto the asphalt and felt for a moment, perhaps, like a gladiator in the Colosseum, taking in the full scale and spectacle of this glorious event from the eye of the storm.

All around them were the sleek bodies of Formula One cars, the sleek bodies of models and drivers, and the gathering crowd of thousands entering the stands. Engines were revving, and the VIPs felt the whirl of their helicopter lifting off to retrieve the next group of valued guests. The air stank of burned rubber and gasoline.

Once on the ground, the VIPs were greeted by a hostess in a golf cart. She wore the tobacco brand on her shirt and hat, and it was emblazoned on the cart. The hostess was cheerful, polite, and attractive. She buzzed them over to the company's hospitality suite, where a champagne lunch had already been set—an all-you-can-smokeand-drink feast attended not only by the VIPs but also two special guests: race car drivers from the team the company was sponsoring.

The dashing drivers would glide into the suite for a moment before the race for a personal hello: big smiles, photo ops, all included in the sponsorship deal.

Let's put this into context in terms of the money behind the deal.

His company had sponsored a decent racing team, with skilled drivers. But unless there was a fluke, they would not be the day's winners; the team might finish third or fourth, if they were lucky. In a way, his company was knowingly paying big money to lose. They were simply not paying enough money to sponsor the likely winner: Ferrari or McLaren.

Marlboro had sponsored Ferrari, and those cars, the most beautiful in the world, were decked out, of course, in the red and white Marlboro colours.

West, a German tobacco brand, had sponsored McLaren.

The cost for sponsoring a third- or fourth-place team was in the multi-million-dollar range. If the company wanted to sponsor Ferrari or McLaren, it could be tens of millions.

Why were tobacco companies spending such ludicrous amounts of money on Grand Prix?

There was no other way to gain that kind of exposure on television. The world was watching.

As the race began, the lawyer watched the VIPs, who in turn watched the cars become blurs of near-supernatural speed. As usual, Ferrari was taking the early lead, putting more and more distance between itself and everybody else.

The lawyer wondered how many of the thousands of people cheering from the grandstands knew that Marlboro was originally a women's brand of cigarette.

When those early studies in the 1950s by Richard Doll were gaining public attention—back before any agreements or directives changed the advertising landscape—Philip Morris had decided to create a cigarette brand that they could market as a safer alternative for male smokers; a manly cigarette, of course, but with a protective measure, a filter.

Until that point, most cigarettes did not have filters.

Instead of creating a new brand from scratch, though, Philip Morris hunted through its basket of existing brands and plucked one out that wasn't performing well. It was easier, and cheaper, to use an existing brand, because, as the lawyer knew too well, it saved the company tens of millions of dollars in legal fees required to secure a new trademark and file international patents.

Once Philip Morris had chosen to resurrect its old women's cigarette brand, Marlboro, there was a challenge: it was precisely because of that new feature—a filter—that the Marlboro rebrand was in danger of still being perceived as "feminine." So, to purposely overcompensate on the macho imagery for the relaunch, it searched for the appropriate symbol that could conjure the inner spirit of the strong American man.

The strategy was to feature different types of "manly men" smoking filtered cigarettes: sailors, soldiers, cowboys, and so on. First up was the cowboy.

As legend had it, the music to match the Marlboro relaunch was suggested by an intern, who went out to the movie *The Magnificent Seven* one night. The story, about men fighting men in the dusty Old West, starring Yul Brynner and Steve McQueen, took place in the rugged landscape of a Mexican village being defended from outlaw-looters by a band of American mercenaries. Spoiler alert: almost everyone in the film dies, but the mercenaries die with "honour" and win the day, because the villagers survive.

After seeing the movie, this kid brought in the music for *The Magnificent Seven* and the agency played it with the cowboy image. The execs loved it, and then everyone loved it. That was the beginning of the Marlboro relaunch campaign, which was anchored on research about what men dreamed of: freedom, nights under the stars by the campfire, and guns. All very macho stuff.

Marlboro became an instant hit, as did their smoking cowboy, and during the 1960s, Philip Morris, with the help of enterprising ad agencies, became adept at experimenting with new marketing initiatives, from sponsoring sophisticated art exhibitions touring the globe to tennis tournaments, music festivals, and, yes, Grand Prix racing.

Gradually, all tobacco companies moved into sponsoring these big cultural and sporting events, helping them grow fast while also growing consumers' awareness of their cigarette brands.

By the 1970s, though, it seemed no tobacco company could catch up to the brand leader: the mighty Marlboro. That refurbished American cigarette went on to become one of the most successful consumer brands in the history of the world.

That was the power of marketing, the lawyer had learned. The perfect campaign could build vast amounts of wealth for a company, and the right advertising agency could transform the image of any given product, no matter its origins or history. Past brand identities could be erased or revised; consumer memories were short.

By the time the lawyer attended British Grand Prix, in 2004, Marlboro still retained its status as one of the most popular brands of cigarette in the US and around the globe, and the brand itself had been valued at more than $20 billion. It was unbeatable, in almost every market.

And because it was the market leader, its parent company could afford to spend tens of millions of dollars sponsoring the winning team of the day: Ferrari, led by Michael Schumacher, the best racing car driver in the world, whose specialty was leaving his competition in the rear-view.

———

The lawyer's company wasn't at Grand Prix to beat Ferrari. Scattered among the pit crews and the crowd were television camera operators, whose images were narrated by broadcast announcers—the storytellers of these contemporary gladiatorial games.

At the same time the Marlboro brand had become mainstream so had television, and the tobacco company was here at Silverstone only because these drivers and their aerodynamic machines were appearing on television sets around the world, watched by tens of millions.

Opportunities for creative brand-building the way Philip Morris had created the Marlboro Man no longer existed. Advertising of tobacco products on television was now generally illegal in most Western countries, and the only way for the lawyer's company to get its brands on television—in front of a national and global audience —was to pour money into events like this one.

Formula One understood this fact very well, and they exploited it by charging the tobacco companies outrageous sums for these sponsorship deals, amounts that were disproportionate to the return on investment, in the lawyer's opinion, and far more than a non-tobacco company would have—or could have—paid.

A non-tobacco company hawking almost any other type of consumer product—a dishwasher detergent or a cola—could simply buy advertising airtime on any show on television, for thousands of dollars. Sponsoring a Formula One team cost millions.

Here's what tobacco companies gained by paying so dearly to put their brands on race cars.

Formula One was an international sport, so it had an audience all around the world. It was a sporting event, but it wasn't exactly an athletic sport. FIFA, for example, would never allow tobacco companies to advertise in their soccer tournaments. Even if it were legal, FIFA would never have gone for it; soccer players and smoking just didn't fit.

The company was left with events like yacht racing, which was high-end; NASCAR, which was a great fit but limited to the US market; bowling and darts, also in the "non-sport sport" category; snooker; and golf.

None of these options was nearly as glamorous as Formula One.

Formula One included very attractive women dressed in racing uniforms, with zippers, and very attractive men who were strapped into ludicrously fast machines.

Even better, the company could brand everything in sight: the drivers, the racing suits, the gloves, the visors, the T-shirts worn by the grid girls strutting around, and, best of all, the gleaming, high performance, aerodynamically superior bodies of the racing cars that made a deafening roar as they passed, over and over again.

The brand was literally driving in circles in front of the thousands of people in the stands and the millions watching on TV.

The lawyer saw it all around him on race day.

Wherever there was space, the company had inserted its brand. And most importantly, from the lawyer's point of view, laws were being respected while doing so.

It got their product on television, and television was still considered the most powerful influence on human consumer behaviour. People saw it on TV and then bought it. It didn't matter how smart you were, or thought you were: if you saw a product on television, you were more inclined to trust it and to pay money for it.

The strangest part of this enormous sponsorship deal: it was impossible for his company to measure its success. The lawyer's company was the top-selling brand in the UK and Ireland, but they had no idea what effect paying for Formula One events had on sales.

"Half the money I spend on advertising is wasted; the trouble is I don't know which half," observed John Wanamaker, a pioneer of marketing at the turn of the twentieth century, and his hundred-year-old admission still held true in this case.

Even so, the lawyer's company was clinging to Grand Prix racing as its last great hope to be on TV. But even as he attended his first race, the lawyer knew there was a guillotine hanging over all of these efforts. His company's marketing department lived in fear of the looming European Union directives, even as they dug their trenches.

Advertising and marketing of consumer products had evolved with the tobacco industry, and from the lawyer's perspective marketing wasn't just about manipulating a product's image or desired audience; it could go deeper than that and involve meaningfully communicating with customers, understanding who they were and how they related to a given product.

Perhaps, at its most sophisticated level, marketing was about creating a dialogue between consumers and their chosen brands. Tobacco companies had been trailblazers in this field, and other manufacturers of consumer products kept an eye on tobacco marketing strategies to copy—or to steal—ideas. In the golden age of smoking, no one was better at selling brand identity than tobacco companies.

In 2004, in the UK, the way in which his company could market its products on home turf was defined by a voluntary self-regulation agreement negotiated between the tobacco companies and the government. So while TV ads were off the table, the voluntary agreement also meant the industry could not do certain other things as well.

Here are a few examples of what the industry had volunteered *not* to do.

The ads the company created couldn't suggest that smoking was linked to any kind of success in life, including, but not limited to, sexual success or athletic success. This meant those ads could not feature attractive men or women being successful at any task. Imagine if Nike had to follow that rule!

Tobacco ads, sensibly, could never target children, so there were restrictions around where the company could place ads. No billboards within one hundred metres of schools; no eye-level advertising in stores frequented by kids; and the types of promotional material created could never be appealing to children.

The voluntary agreement had been one way for the industry to continue to advertise its products to adults, with a certain level of discretion. And as the lawyer was taught, not following the agreement could lead to further regulations, which was exactly what the company didn't want. It was the reason any major company took part in a voluntary agreement: to avoid more laws and regulations like the EU directives.

Where the industry *did* want to be, and where marketing was still flexing considerable muscle, was at point of sale. So drive teams were desperately important; he could see their value more clearly now. Having the brands glowing in vending machines in bars and showcased prominently in convenience stores was indescribably valuable as restrictions increased in other arenas.

Sampling was still happening, meaning teams of people would go out and give away free product at clubs and bars as a strategy to get smokers to switch brands. Those teams, of course, had to be sure they were complying with the law, so obviously there was no giving free cigarettes to children or teenagers. It happened at establishments catering to the over-eighteen crowd where ID was required to get in.

Sometimes, those teams would offer pack swaps: they'd ask if someone was a smoker, and if so offer to trade that person's pack for a full pack of one of the company's brands—right out of Ben's playbook. And while you were out there dealing with customers face to face, why not ask them for their contact information?

Direct mail was communications gold for a time. This was about getting adult smokers to show their ID and voluntarily give away their address and then asking them to tick a box on a form which indicated they'd be very happy if the company communicated with them by mail. Every tobacco company was doing this, and it was effective.

Still, in the midst of all of this bobbing and weaving by the marketing department, they keenly understood that with a European Union directive specifically designed to paralyze tobacco company marketing efforts, all of their campaigns might soon be impossible. The directive had been created but not yet been implemented in the UK. The blade of the guillotine had been raised, ready to drop.

This meant that even as the lawyer joined the company and learned about their powerful arsenal of marketing and advertising strategies, he was aware that at some point in the very near future all these efforts could become a piece of advertising history destined for a museum of consumer culture history.

It did take a few years, but in 2005 the EU directive was implemented in the UK—and it was far worse than the company had imagined.

As promised, that directive banned most forms of advertising for tobacco companies. But the UK government decided to use this opportunity to push the spirit of the directive further and banned all forms of cigarette advertisements, with no exceptions.

Overnight, decades of communications with customers, both directly and indirectly, simply shut down. Silence.

Iconic advertising campaigns that were cutting-edge by any standard were simply thrown away. Tobacco, which had been an innovator in the fields of marketing, communication, and advertising, could suddenly no longer reach out to its customers.

At his office—as at tobacco offices across the UK, he guessed—marketing staff were delivered pink slips. The curtain came down, and much of the department was simply sent home. The same thing happened at advertising agencies with big tobacco accounts. This really was like no other consumer product.

So, just over fifty years after Richard Doll and Austin Bradford Hill released their groundbreaking research, the anti-smoking wave had finally crashed with force into the United Kingdom. Doll, no doubt, was pleased to see this happen, just months before he passed away in 2005. After all, it had only taken half a century to score this major victory against Big Tobacco's marketing muscle on this side of the Atlantic.

What the company still had was the rest of the world, outside of Western Europe and the US, and, for a short period of time, this Grand Prix circuit, which was protected under a unique international jurisdiction that fell outside the new laws.

Thank god, the company could still pour money into this televised race, and Formula One was very happy to take that money.

Let's get back to the champagne lunch.

The VIP guests had been placed right inside the spectacle, in a secure area directly below the grandstand. Waiters in black tie served them as the cars screamed around the track and the fine china plates and stemware trembled on the tables.

When lunch was finished, they were escorted to reserved seating at an exclusive grandstand. And for a few lucky customers, there was a chance to go down and tour the racing pits and the garages where the drivers and crew were hanging out. This experience became a story to tell their grandkids about at Christmas—at every Christmas.

After Ferrari had won the race, VIPs were invited, in true English style, for scones, clotted cream, and tea. The purpose was to slow down the exit process so that not everyone wanted to get on the helicopter at the same time.

The chopper came and went for the next hour and a half. At the other end was each VIP's limousine driver, who had been sitting there all day outside the barn watching the grass grow. It was not a late evening; everyone had a good time and was home by 5 P.M. for dinner.

Over the next few years, the lawyer was lucky enough to attend Grand Prix races in Belgium, France, Germany, Italy, Monaco, San Marino, Spain, the US, and Canada too.

In 2006, another European Union directive aimed at tobacco companies was fully implemented, and this time the industry was ordered by law to no longer sponsor Formula One races. Fast cars and big tobacco had found the perfect marketing relationship for a time—and then it was over.

Share prices in tobacco companies should have plummeted once those EU directives were implemented, but they kept going up. Why?

WINNING IN KAZAKHSTAN

One day at HQ in London, circa 2004, Mary handed him the file for Central Asia: Kyrgyzstan, Uzbekistan, Turkmenistan, Armenia, Mongolia, and Kazakhstan. She informed the lawyer, who was still moving up the ranks, that he was now responsible for a landmass that included anything east of Turkey, south of Russia, west of China, and north of India.

These were growth markets. Translation: more people were smoking more, not less, in these countries, despite the still-expanding waves from the surgeon general's report.

The biggest growth, and bulk of the money in this file, was in Kazakhstan, and much of that surge was due to an ingenious move by the company's marketing department to leverage British pop culture in the wave of anti-Americanism that was sweeping Eastern Europe after 9/11 and the ensuing US invasion of Iraq. The effort had all been about pushing one particular brand, and it had worked.

———

The company prepped him for his first trip there.

This wasn't like going to Ireland to tour a factory, or to Spain, or to any other part of Western Europe. For this trip, he was injected with immunization shots, given a first aid kit with instructions and with drugs—for example, codeine—and provided with a security briefing from a company called Control Risk.

Control Risk forwarded him a list of local telephone numbers of people to call—fixers who worked for a local security firm. They also gave him a lock for his hotel room door, a big clamp he was taught how to use. So they didn't trust the security at the hotels. Reassuring.

There was another dimension to his general feeling of nervousness around this particular journey: his wife was pregnant. Her punchline when updating friends with the exciting news was this: "His contribution to this outcome was brief." Thank god she still made him laugh.

All joking aside, he felt extremely unsure about leaving her at this moment—working against powerful biological instincts, travelling to a far-off place while his wife stayed home to nurture and protect their unborn child.

At least he'd be able to contact her whenever he chose. He was issued a mobile phone that would work in that part of the world. This was pre-iPhone, after all, and the super-phone they gave him was the size of a brick. And, of course, he packed his man from Del Monte suits, his hero-abroad costume.

He travelled to Kazakhstan, but this time Mary came with him. She was still his superior and, he hoped, his sworn protector. Actually, it was her first time visiting as well. They flew from Heathrow, on British Airways, and were the only customers flying in business class. The business-class seats were the older cradle-style seats; travelling to New York, you'd get the new flatbed model. This was like stepping back in time.

Their flight touched down in Yekaterinburg, on the edge of Siberia, to refuel. Passengers were told not to get off the plane. But because he was a business-class passenger, he was given special treatment and allowed to stand at the door of the airplane and smoke a cigarette. Thank god. Now that his wife was pregnant, he could smoke again.

He pulled out his phone, but there was no signal.

He looked around. It was mountainous: the Ural Mountains. There was snow on the ground. It was an epic sight, and he relished the moment, smoking while looking out at this strange new place from the plane.

What stuck in his mind were the old Soviet-era vehicles and planes parked on the airport field. He'd never seen those designs before. This was Cold War machinery: sixty years old—clunky, supersized—out of a spy movie. Everything looked fierce. The planes seemed bigger than normal, huge metal beasts with engines in the wrong places, wings in the wrong places. It looked like alien technology to him.

While he smoked, he noticed that the guy refuelling the plane was smoking as well. Where the fuck was he? he thought.

He suddenly got a signal on his phone, so he made a call to get his voice messages. One of them was from the president of an American tobacco company. He called him right there from outside the plane, staring at the Urals.

"Where are you?" the president asked.

"I think I'm somewhere in Siberia."

"Who did you piss off?" laughed the president.

Back inside the plane, he was in the good old corporate bubble. Mary had an entire row to herself, and she'd stretched out and fallen asleep. She remained asleep when the plane lifted off for Almaty, their destination.

———

They landed in Almaty at about 4 A.M., local time: still dark.

This was new for him as well. He'd never landed at such an early hour—totally outside the boundaries of normal social activity. The plane parked on the airfield, steps were rolled out, and they descended onto the tarmac. He noticed a Lufthansa plane parked nearby. The familiar branding, even in the darkness, was comforting.

Most of the passengers got on a bus, but a separate minivan pulled up for them. A man got out with a chalkboard sign with the lawyer's and Mary's names written on it. The minivan took them to a private screening station, where they were waved through. They had needed Kazakh visas, which the company had arranged.

A car took them to a VIP arrival terminal, where Beck, the head of the company's legal department in Kazakh, was—at this very surreal late-early hour—waiting for them. Their visit was a big deal; Beck's suit looked freshly pressed, and he was driving a new Ford sedan, which to him was probably like having a Porsche. He was not alone, though.

Beck wanted to take them to the hotel in his Ford, but another man was there as well, and he was driving an SUV with bulletproof glass. The two had a terse exchange in Kazakh. The armoured-car guy was insisting that he take the lawyers; this was company protocol. Eventually, the lawyer and Mary got into the bulletproof SUV.

It was still dark out as they cruised into Almaty, wrapped safely in their armour. At the hotel, reception was expecting them. The rooms were paid for, of course. The hotel was a Western chain and billed as four stars, but, just like the cradle seats on the plane, it felt like this place hadn't been renovated since the 1980s.

After they checked in, Beck, who had followed closely behind in his shining Ford, advised his guests to go to bed. He said they'd be picked up at 10 A.M. So the lawyer went to sleep. Then up, for a cold shower, brownish water. He turned on the television, but there were no English channels.

He examined the room: cigarette burn marks on the carpets, on the chairs. This was the deluxe room. The towels were frayed; the mini-bar had an orange soda with a smiling boy on the label. There were no brands he recognized.

He and Mary met downstairs around 9:40 A.M. for breakfast. The buffet, in terms of quality, reminded him of a cheap hotel on the Vegas strip. They had croissants, but they were covered in a glaze of sugar. There were more brands of warm soda he didn't recognize. He stuck to black coffee.

He'd been warned ahead of time to bring food, and he had: a case of peanut butter sandwich crackers. Each plastic-wrapped packet had six sandwiches. So that's what he ate pretty much the entire time he was there. Boy was he happy he'd brought them.

When they got back into the armoured SUV, he realized that the driver hadn't left the hotel; he'd just sat there, waiting for them, while they slept.

The drive to the factory was about thirty minutes.

They passed row upon row of Soviet-style housing blocks. It felt grim, but there was no traffic. The roads were clear, and they drove very fast. A lot of people were standing on the side of the road, thumbing rides. In Kazakh, it was totally normal for people to share rides and split gas; every car was public transport, just like in much of the old Soviet empire. This was Eastern European Uber, way before Uber existed.

He pointed to a dead dog on the road, but Mary missed it. Then he pointed to another dead dog. She saw that one. It was a golden retriever, the big dog just lying there on its back on the side of the road.

Then he saw it: a human body. It looked dead to him, half on the sidewalk, half in the gutter. Hard to know if the person was alive or gone, but they didn't seem to be moving.

"Should we stop?" he asked the driver.

"No stopping," the driver said.

They did stop, though—twice—for police who were taking "tolls," five to ten US dollars at a time. Their driver paid, no argument.

They arrived at the factory compound, the gates opened, and they were transported into a modern factory complex in the middle of Kazakhstan, including new roads, a flagpole, and new buildings. There was a bit of a space station feel to it. With surprisingly few people in sight, it almost felt unsafe.

Beck directed them straight to the executive offices, where they drank more coffee and had a chat with the English-speaking expats. These men were tough corporate wanderers; they were here to build the business and to serve the needs of the tobacco empire in an uncorporate environment just past the edge of the Western world.

The group was not happy to see management from HQ. They had this look on their faces, as if to say, "This is not like the legal department from back home." In his company, these men were the toughest pirates on the corporate vessel.

Then a factory tour. It could have been anywhere, though frankly it looked much more modern than the manufacturing facilities in Northern Ireland, with more new tech. And in Almaty they couldn't make the product fast enough: the machines were humming twenty-four hours a day—no slowdowns, no closures.

Business was going so well, the factory was being expanded. Sticks made here were supplying the entire region: all those post-Soviet growth markets—"the Stans"—now open to Western investment, plus Mongolia, Armenia, and a trickle headed to China.

Kazakhstan wasn't a place where you just built a factory. It was three times as expensive to undertake here as it was in the UK. All the materials had to be imported. But if a person were led here blindfolded and taken on a tour of the factory, they would never know they were in Kazakhstan. Even the electrical plugs were British.

The purpose of the factory was to churn out cigarettes cheaply that were no different from a British-made brand; it was less expensive to produce it here rather than import it. And locals here craved foreign product. They liked drinking Coke and eating Oreo cookies. And they enjoyed smoking British cigarettes.

What most Kazakhs probably didn't realize was that these products—cola, cookies, and cigarettes—were not made in the US or the UK; they were made under licensing agreements in Kazakhstan, by Kazakhs. The brand you bought often had little to do with the place where the product was made. File under Global Consumer Illusions.

The lawyer did his job. He plugged in his laptop and used the overhead projector to entertain his new audience, delivering his legal presentation on that first day, bleary-eyed and jet-lagged.

It was about global marketing standards, the importance of regulation, and following corporate policy.

No one argued with him, but there was one man in the room who looked at the lawyer throughout his presentation as if he was a corporate muppet. "Fuck you, go home." That's what this guy's look said.

These executives were expats in the real sense, living way outside the typical corporate comfort zone to fill the company coffers, and to make themselves a lot of money as well—small fortunes, really.

The lawyer was young, he looked young, and he had his babysitter, Mary, in the room with him—and she was the only woman in the room. He noted the entire audience here was comprised of men. Just like the windows of their armoured SUV, the glass ceiling here in Kazakhstan seemed to be bulletproof.

To this grizzled crew, the two visitors were just drones who had been dispatched from head office to remind everyone there were rules here too in the Wild East. The way to make money wasn't to break rules; it was to steal Kazakh customers from other international cigarette brands.

That's exactly what these expat corporate pirates were doing so well. They were stealing the nation's business, and, frankly, everyone was smoking better cigarettes because of their efforts. They were stealing business from other companies, including Western companies. Most notably, they were stealing business from Philip Morris, makers of the mighty Marlboro.

He had enough experience giving presentations to know that going in with an all-guns-blazing approach wouldn't go down well with the expats, so he softened it. The backbone of the presentation was an introduction to the impending tobacco regulations in Europe and what those implications meant for the Kazakh market.

Things were changing fast, even here, and new restrictions would be coming into play. Here's a three-line summary of his talk: There were rules in place and the company had to follow them. If it didn't follow the rules, it could get into serious trouble. It didn't want to get into trouble; it wanted to make a lot of money.

In essence, he was showing them the battles that the company had lost recently—some big ones—and a few small battles that the company was winning. Either way, though, the progression of tobacco legislation moved from west to east: that was the undeniable pattern.

There was good news, though.

The GDP of Kazakhstan was set to get higher, per capita. This was a country that was changing. It still felt pain from the fall of communism and its separation from the Soviet empire—which had occurred only in 1991—but the country was larger in geographical size than all of Western Europe put together. It was enormous. And thanks to the efforts of these expats, the company had gained a monster share of this new, growing market.

The expats still weren't interested, but the lawyer did his best to stay on point, and to sound enthusiastic.

After the presentation, they had a fairly normal working day and ate lunch in the factory canteen. The food on offer was some kind of mystery meat. He ate his peanut butter crackers instead, drank six bottles of imported water over the course of the day, and smoked a lot.

On that first evening after work, he and Mary were taken back to the hotel and given a couple of hours to rest. Then they were picked up by two of the expat executives and driven to a Chinese restaurant with English menus for dinner. He noticed there were no prices on these tourist menus.

The execs didn't talk business; they talked about their lives as expats.

They were reluctant to discuss how much money they were making, but they did talk about how their families were affected, particularly in a place where they couldn't drive alone and where their wives weren't allowed to drive at all. Basically, they lived out their days on a residential compound—the space station lifestyle. Both of the execs turned out to be Canadian, so, of course, they talked a little about hockey.

He knew they were making a lot of money, certainly, with expat salary benefits and bonuses, but life was not easy. They felt displaced, and the lawyer thought they looked tired and sort of unhealthy. The food was ordered, and to his surprise, when it arrived, it was fantastic. He ate a lot of that Chinese food. The bill was taken care of, but he did get a look at it; it was probably the most expensive Chinese food he's ever had. It wasn't a late night.

When he and Mary were dropped off at the hotel, they went into the bar for a couple of drinks. They were both really jet-lagged.

The bar was interesting. There were a lot of women, but Mary was the only one there who looked like a business type. It took a few minutes for it to sink in, but many of the other women at the bar seemed to be prostitutes. Most of the men were Western, and most of them were smoking. They had that "we're working on an oil rig" look.

These weren't suited executives; they were rougher, they were getting hammered, and a lot of them were negotiating prices with the local women. As he sat with Mary, prostitutes came up to him and were writing down their price on pieces of paper.

The women—some of them seemed more like girls—didn't seem to understand how much money these mostly Western expats had at their disposal, and in his opinion they were negotiating very low prices. He and Mary could hear the prices being discussed; no one was pretending to be doing anything else or keeping their voices down. Mary looked disgusted. Some of the conversations got into some serious detail, negotiating sexual acts to be performed.

"I want anal."

"Okay, fine. Twenty dollars."

That kind of stuff.

The lawyer looked at Mary and raised an eyebrow.

"For twenty bucks, I might have a go," he joked, trying to break the grimness of the situation.

Mary was not amused, and he didn't blame her. It wasn't funny at all. It was absolutely chilling.

The bar was surrounded by a courtyard with indoor fountains and elevator banks, and the elevators were glass. He and Mary sipped their drinks and watched the men and the girls walking to the elevators together, then rising up out of sight in their glass boxes. Basically, they were staying at a brothel, he thought.

Thank god the rooms had thick walls, so he couldn't hear a thing. The balcony door didn't lock properly in his room, and he installed the clamp on the door as instructed. But even though he was high up, and he had the clamp on the door, he never felt safe there. In fact, he never really felt safe during the whole trip.

In the morning, when he woke up, he felt very far from home. He'd been spoiled, had spent a lot of time in luxury land, at the finest restaurants, beaches, clubs, galleries, and hotels. Grand Prix races, yachts in Monaco, the very best of Western Europe.

When he and Mary were ready to head back to the factory, their SUV driver was there at the hotel again. In fact, over the course of their stay, he was always there, watching over them, and yet somehow he managed to change and shave. It was an international hygienic mystery.

The lawyer understood exactly why the expats weren't even pretending to be interested in his presentation. They didn't need to be interested. They were winning the tobacco war here, and they knew it.

These executives were the wizards behind an ingenious marketing strategy that had become legend inside his company. They'd managed to take over the Kazakh cigarette market in a matter of months through an unlikely branding and promotional coup, while using one of the shittiest brands the company had.

Sovereign was created in the 1800s, and in the UK it was virtually dead as a brand. Grandmothers smoked that brand of cigarette; men who were chain-smoking shut-ins smoked that brand. No one under sixty years old sought it out in the UK. In London, it was the opposite of cool and quite possibly had never been cool there.

But in Kazakhstan, Sovereign had come to represent the height of British chic and was the number one selling brand.

How had these execs pulled off that magic trick?

It all started with London Routemaster buses.

Remember those big red double-decker buses? Those clunkers were being phased out by London's mayor, Ken Livingstone. Yes, the city had kept some of them running to appease the tourists, but basically the buses were being sold off, and at fantastically low prices. Who would want them?

His tobacco company saw an opportunity. It could use those buses to export British culture—to sell cigarettes. So they bought a bunch of them, then shipped them out there. The lawyer liked to imagine, though, that a crew of guys had driven those crazy-looking things all the way out to Kazakhstan. What a road trip that would have been: imagine cruising through the epic post-Soviet landscapes of Eastern Europe all the way to Almaty—in these honking red buses: the journey was more than six thousand kilometres.

Once in Almaty, they smothered the double-decker buses with branding for Sovereign, transforming them into giant red advertising billboards on wheels.

The buses were used as mobile hubs to hand out promotional materials and free samples of the brand to the populace. The company had started selling this brand here from nothing, but the buses worked. Kazakhs found them fun. The company started buying black London taxis as well, and they shipped them out here too.

It's hard to imagine, but for months in Almaty there were all these red London buses and black cabs cruising around the city, handing out free British cigarettes.

The Routemasters and the taxis were an important component of the campaign, but it was more sophisticated than a bunch of old buses and cars with branding. Back in the West, in tourist markets where it was still legal, the company was giving away T-shirts or beach towels to market cigarettes—sometimes a free bottle of booze. Free booze with cartons of cigarettes sounds great, right?

Here, though, each pack of cigarettes came with branded dollars—a form of cash the company created specifically for this growth market.

When a customer opened a pack of the company's cigarettes, the pack was giving them something in return, above and beyond the sticks: Monopoly money, basically. Branded money. Except this fake money became valuable, because smokers could redeem it for real items.

If a Kazakh smoked enough cigarettes, they could save their brand money and trade it in for a coffee maker or, if they saved enough of it, a fridge.

In a way, it became economically advantageous to smoke: a Kazakh could theoretically live a better lifestyle with the prizes bought with fake money from their cigarette purchases. The company was giving people what they desired: upgraded cutlery, linens, small appliances—important household items that could be acquired with cigarette dollars.

And the prizes became more grandiose: at one point the company started giving away cars.

To be realistic, one person would have to smoke four packs a day for a hundred years to get that car, but there was strength in numbers. A situation developed where communities of families started to pool their branded dollars. It required an "it takes a village" kind of approach. But having that car could be life-changing.

From that perspective, smoking cigarettes actually helped the community. Everything was upside down here.

The brand took off, and suddenly it was everywhere. And the cigarette dollars became more valuable than just funny money. Beck told the lawyer that so many people were using the company's fake currency that at one point it was considered more valuable than the legitimate Kazakh currency.

The lawyer had never seen anything like this model—and there were more pieces to it.

———

The day after the lawyer's presentation, Beck escorted him and Mary on a market tour of Almaty.

The purpose was for the lawyer to observe how the product was sold here so he could better assist Beck from head office in the UK.

The team went out in two SUVs, black Toyotas or Hondas. The door panels around the ashtrays were scarred with cigarette burns, but the cars were far nicer than any of the other vehicles on the street. He got into one with Beck and Mary, and in the other were some of the local sales guys, who didn't speak English. He never even conversed with them.

They spent a whole day cruising around Almaty, stopping at grocery stores, gas stations, bars, and restaurants, and at stands by the side of the road.

Kazakhstan was a unique place to sell cigarettes for many reasons.

It was a Central Asian market that was starting to mature, a resource-rich country with massive oil reserves. As a result, Kazakhs' quality of life was reported to be improving dramatically and the middle class was growing—but the country's Soviet past was obvious.

The state of the roads was impressive, and in every direction the lawyer saw buildings with the hammer-and-sickle insignia stamped into the stone, statues of Lenin and other Soviet heroes. He'd been to Moscow, and recognized the epic scale and the raw, brutalist aesthetic of Soviet-era city planning: those huge public squares, wide streets, and monolithic apartment blocks. This definitely wasn't like taking in the majestic sight of the Kremlin, though; many of these Kazakh apartment blocks looked like they were about to crumble.

Another Soviet influence: an extraordinary number of military and government personnel were on the streets and in public places, and a lot of them wore the peaked military caps that looked sort of like pizzas. If you've seen the movie *Borat*, you know that hat—

almost like the kind of hat a pirate would wear, except the crown at the back was too big.

What he found unnerving were the stops: police, military, or bandits, all had set up official-looking but unsanctioned toll booths. Their driver was routinely handing out anywhere from one to five US dollars every time they were stopped. The payouts were completely normal, part of getting around. If you wanted to move inside the corporate bubble here, you had to open your wallet. This was pay to play, Kazakh style.

And a lot of people were smoking, a lot of the time, everywhere they went. The only time he'd seen cigarettes retailed in an environment where they were treated no differently from other products, like bottled water, chips, or cola, was on the Canary Islands, but this was a substantially larger market. Cigarettes were piled high like any other consumer good, and sold cheap.

Health warnings on packs were not mandated in Kazakhstan at this point. But that didn't mean the company wasn't putting health warnings on their product all the same.

It might have been perfectly legal to give cigarettes to kids, but they were not doing this either; it had to be eighteen years or older. Don't mess around: that was the lawyer's message to Beck and the expat corporate pirates.

What made Kazakhstan such an opportunity for his company, and the reason they were prepared to make big investments here, was that this was a totally new market for his Western company, and it was massive. Almost twenty million people, with a growing slice of disposable income in this "Stan" alone, but when you included all those post-Soviet Central Asia countries, it was a population of north of sixty million and growing.

The rules of the West were coming—as he'd indicated in his presentation—but they hadn't yet arrived in full force. The transition from

Soviet communism to Western capitalism was a work-in-progress, while the concept of American exceptionalism was greeted here by post-Soviet skepticism coupled with suspicion around the circumstances of the US-led Iraq War—so there was an extra opportunity for brands from the West that weren't star-spangled.

His company had been intentionally mixing British pop culture into Kazakh culture to its advantage, he was told by the team. This approach was similar to what the Americans had managed to do in Europe in the 1940s and then in Asia in the 1950s. And in the same way that Coca-Cola had been established as the crown jewel of fizzy beverage ambassadors at an international level, the mighty Marlboro, of course, had held that spot in the cigarette brand hierarchy. In virtually every other foreign market, Marlboro was indeed the leader—yet not in this market, not during his visit.

Marlboro, in fact, was in third place, because these old English brands were kicking everyone's butt.

It became clear on the market tour that Beck was proud of the work the company was accomplishing in Almaty. He took them to as many points of sale and distribution that he could in the space of a day. It was manic. The lawyer, still jet-lagged, would have been happy seeing two or three examples. All he did that day was look at whatever Beck showed him, and smoke cigarette after cigarette inside the SUV. He saw more points of sale than he'd seen in his life.

Beck was adamant. They went to gas stations, grocery stores, bars and restaurants, street and market vendors, and not just in Almaty. At one point they were about 160 kilometres from the border with China. The lawyer hadn't even known that Kazakhstan bordered China.

He witnessed, on several occasions, retailers selling loose cigarettes from packs of twenty. This was normal in Kazakh, Beck told him. In Europe and America, it would have been treated as a petty crime.

Perhaps most shocking was the sale of cigarettes in individual little plastic tubes, one cigarette at a time.

The lawyer noted that people seemed to look older here. It was tough terrain, and life did not seem easy. Apparently, locals did go on vacation, though. He saw advertisements everywhere for vacation spots. India and Turkey seemed popular, both of which were short flights away.

He also noticed that a lot of major Western companies had already established themselves in this market, from gas station brands to colas to potato chips. Even so, he'd never been in a place like this before where he couldn't plainly see the lines that delineated the tourist-friendly zones, and so he stayed safely inside the company's corporate bubble.

Towards the end of the day, Beck brought them to Surrey House.

At the conceptual centre of the tobacco company's marketing campaign was the creation of Surrey House, which was a reference to the leafy county just outside London where stockbrokers and lawyers lived—as well as a handful of Russian oligarchs, apparently. Of course, there was no *actual* historic manor near London called Surrey House. It was a pretentious conceit—a vibe that was based on the idea of upper-crust Englishness.

When Beck pulled up to Surrey House, the lawyer couldn't believe what he was looking at. Standing before them was a replica of an English mansion that sort of looked like it could have been in Surrey except it had been built in the parking lot of an Almaty shopping plaza, next to a gas station.

Surrey House may have been an odd piece of architectural fiction, but all of those real prizes at the heart of the company's marketing campaign were distributed from here. It was from the old Sears catalogue and distribution centre playbook: when a Kazakh smoker wanted to claim their treasure with their branded tobacco currency, they made the pilgrimage to Surrey House.

With Mary and Beck, he gazed at the little English manor nestled in the parking lot. He really felt he was in a strange land on the other side of the world. It was a surreal moment—truly absurd—and he tried to savour the strangeness of it all. Beck seemed very pleased.

Beck was one of the few people he had crossed paths with in life of whom he truly thought, This guy is special.

It was odd, because they'd just met and were from opposite sides of the world, but the lawyer felt a connection to this Kazakh man.

Beck was a Muslim, wore a beard, and was older than the lawyer by at least ten to fifteen years, so was somewhere in his forties. He'd grown up under the Russians and was proud of his Kazakh heritage and traditions.

He was into horses, which was not surprising; many Kazakhs lived and died by the horse. They ate their horses, and they traded their horses. Horses were transportation; they were a commodity; and they were a symbol of national pride.

During Soviet rule, Beck had become a dissident. He told the lawyer he'd refused to serve in the Russian military and was therefore separated from his family and sent to Siberia, where he was forced into labour. Now, he'd been reunited with them, had a solid job as a lawyer working for a major tobacco company, and was cruising Almaty in his new Ford making a steady salary. In a way, Beck was an example of the growing middle class that Western companies touted as the future when they pitched investing here.

Beck eventually invited the lawyer to his home, and the lawyer was shocked when he saw where his colleague lived. This man was the head lawyer for a giant tobacco company in Kazakhstan, but he lived in a Soviet-style apartment block and was obviously being paid a local's salary.

At the apartment, Beck introduced the lawyer to his teenage daughter. He could instantly see she was falling for all the trappings of the West and veering far away from the traditions Beck was so proud of. She looked like an MTV girl and was interested in New Kids on the Block. So much for anti-Americanism; it didn't seem to have affected Kazakhstan's teen-girl population or New Kids' album sales.

Beck obviously felt some affection for the lawyer. He wanted to show the lawyer as much as he could of his country, not just the tobacco market. He seemed to have a genuine desire to share Kazakh culture, including eating a traditional Kazakh dinner, which they did—and which led to the lawyer's experience of the sheep's head.

On their last night in Kazakhstan, Beck met the lawyer and Mary in the hotel lobby, and the armoured SUV drove them to the outskirts of Almaty.

About half an hour later, they pulled up to what seemed like a park surrounded by trees. In the clearing, set back from the road, was a big tent—almost like a circus tent, but not as playfully coloured. It was a very large tent, though, which they entered together. It felt sort of magical.

Inside, the tent was quite spacious, and divided into rooms. There was no floor, but carpets had been laid down on the grass. The host led them through a series of tent-rooms and seated them at a "table." The table consisted of a large, round wooden top set on the ground over the carpet.

The lawyer and Mary followed Beck's lead, and they all sat down on the carpet around the wooden surface. This was a ceremonial meal, Beck explained, and he directed it to start by clapping his hands. A crew of five young women—girls, really—suddenly appeared. The girls were dressed in traditional Kazakh dance costume: dark burgundy and tassels. They gathered around them, forming a near circle.

There were five in the group having dinner at the table, and each guest was served by one of the girls.

The dinner started with a hot towel. The girl acting as the lawyer's server gave him his towel and stood immediately behind him. He suddenly felt her hands on his shoulders, and she began kneading them, and then his back. Surprised, he looked over at Mary. Mary had declined that experience.

Then a large silver bowl arrived, filled with ice and a few bottles of vodka.

Beck filled their glasses and explained that the meal they were being served was a regional specialty. He gave a toast. Their glasses of vodka were refilled. And then Beck clapped again and the food started arriving.

The first course was in individual bowls placed in front of each guest. The lawyer looked inside his bowls. Well, it looked like semen. Beck explained that what the lawyer was looking at was yak's milk and, in a second bowl, camel's milk—both fermented.

Mary smiled. "Try it," she said playfully to the lawyer.

He lifted the bowl up and took a sip. It was warm. It was like sour buttermilk with gristly bits in it.

The lawyer nodded. "It's very nice," he said to Beck.

Everyone at the table downed the contents of their bowls, except for the lawyer and Mary.

"If you're not going to finish those, we will," Beck said.

The lawyer happily gave Beck his two bowls.

Most of the dishes from then on were served family style, carried out on platters and placed in the middle of the "table," with each girl serving a portion to her respective guest. Then the next course, and the next. And they kept on coming. It turned out they'd sat down for a ten-course meal.

Here were some of the courses he remembered.

A plate of sliced meat. Beck explained to them that it was an entire horse penis—and that it was a delicacy. This sounded improbable, and yet there it was. Beck explained, "You eat horse penis in the West, but they don't tell you."

The lawyer tried it; Mary did not.

There was a dish that seemed to consist of yellowed horse fat. This was pieces of horse fat that had been spiced, its yellow tinge a result of it having been aged or something. And it was *just* fat. Even if you ate pancetta, there *was* meat with it. The fat was served with bread. You spread the fat on the bread and ate. He tried that too.

There was an excellent salad, thank god—with cucumber and other local produce. The vegetables were crisp and delicious.

Then another tough one: prairie oysters, or testicles. He didn't know if they were horse testicles or bull testicles. He didn't eat them; this was his limit. Mary wasn't game for that course either.

The next course was called five fingers. It was a Kazakh specialty of rice noodles covered in bits of tripe and other pieces of meat. The problem was that to him it smelled like a dog that hadn't been washed. It was truly awful. He wasn't squeamish, but this was a challenge.

When the main course was served, it turned out to be the most delicious roasted lamb he'd ever had, served with roasted potatoes and green beans. They brought the whole lamb, which was stuffed, to the table, and carved it in front of the group. It was superb—nothing like the overcooked British pub-lunch lamb on Sunday. Each diner was given various cuts, stuffed with garlic, tender inside and crispy outside. The green beans had a wonderful dill sauce. The lawyer was grateful, and so was Mary.

The vodka was making Mary move slow; Beck was drinking very little; and the lawyer was drinking more than either of them. He had to wash down all those courses with something.

There were a couple of desserts, two or three was his guess, but things were getting kind of hazy by that point.

They made small talk during the meal, and during the conversation the lawyer revealed that his wife was expecting a child in four or five months.

Beck lit up.

He explained that because the lawyer and his wife were expecting, their group needed to conduct a special ceremony—for the health of the future baby and the prosperity of the lawyer's family.

Beck clapped, and one of the girls came over immediately. The two had a quick exchange in Kazakh. She showed she understood and went away.

About fifteen minutes later, two girls brought out a giant board with something on it under tin foil and with flowers visible around the edge. It looked as if one of the girls had just gone out into the park and picked them. The girls took off the tin foil, and on top of the fresh flowers was the entire steaming boiled head of a sheep.

For those who have never had the pleasure of seeing an entire boiled sheep's head on a platter, it is not large. It wasn't small either, but it was not as big as he might have expected. It was, though, a sheep's head—clearly.

It had been skinned and boiled, and there it was in front of him on the board.

Beside it was a very long knife.

"We have a special ceremony, and you need to follow these steps," Beck explained to the lawyer.

The lawyer hesitantly agreed.

"You have to cut off the ears first."

Steam was coming off the head. The lawyer picked up the knife and sliced off each ear. He put the ears on the platter, as directed by Beck.

He was instructed to cut off the nose, which he did. He sliced right through it; wow, that knife was sharp. The nose was placed on the platter.

They pried open the sheep's mouth. Beck told him to cut out the tongue. He did so, and put the tongue on the platter too, beside the ears. Then Beck instructed him to gouge the eyes out. He stuck the knife in around the eyes and sort of popped them out, and put them on the platter.

Beck clapped, and one of the girls came over.

She had with her a small vise, and she inserted the vise into the skull and pried open the top of the skull. The lawyer was asked to scoop out the brains. They came out, kind of oozy, and he dumped a little pile of hot brains on the platter.

And then the two girls took away what remained of the head.

Mary was smiling, and so was the lawyer.

"Now you eat," Beck said. "In order for your baby to be fully blessed and healthy, you have to eat what you cut off the lamb."

He said this in his matter-of-fact way with a completely straight face.

The lawyer thought about his options.

"Out of respect for your tradition," he answered carefully, "I will sample a piece of each."

But he did not eat any of those brains. And he didn't eat the eyes —there was a limit. And, yes, the vodka helped.

He was grateful Mary took photographs, so he had proof of their gastronomical adventure.

———

The lawyer and Mary got up early the next morning and the driver took them to the airport for the flight home. They arrived at the airport about three hours before the flight.

Normally, when he travelled internationally, he'd head for business-class check-in. But this airport didn't allow for that. You had to go through emigration first before you went to the check-in desk.

The lawyer provided his documents, passport, and ticket chits. He didn't understand what they were doing with his documents. There was a lot of looking, staring silently at the documents as if he'd done something wrong, then looking blankly at him.

There was zero VIP treatment.

After that, they checked in at the British Airways desk, then had to go through another document control station to officially leave the country. Again, it was two or three minutes of someone examining his passport and saying nothing. When they got into the area for their departure gate, there were no shops or anything, just an airline lounge with a cloud of smoke. It was too much even for a smoker like him. They walked into the lounge, looked around for a second, and walked out.

So they sat outside the gate awaiting departure. He ate a Snickers he'd taken from the hotel mini-bar.

When they boarded, he had the instantaneous feeling of being back in Britain: *click*. He was home even before they took off. Tea and coffee were served with that wonderful, understated elegance of British Airways inflight service.

He visited Kazakhstan only a handful of times after that. The company tried to replicate the basics of that Kazakh marketing campaign in other Central Asian markets, but it never had the same success anywhere else. What happened in Kazakhstan remained for many years the company's most successful example of an international marketing campaign.

His takeaway from that trip: hallelujah—it was possible to beat the mighty Marlboro in a foreign market. Seize the marketing moment, because it might never come again.

A few months later, he and his wife welcomed their healthy baby daughter into the world. She was a joy—although he was bleary-eyed when he arrived at the office on many mornings in that first year as a parent.

Back at HQ in London, he was also delivered a new addition to his communications toolbox: a Blackberry. He accepted the Canadian-made invention with a mixture of pride and fear. Senior lawyers were issued the devices specifically so they could monitor email outside of the office, but also outside office hours. Up until this point, when away from HQ—or even just at home having dinner—he was reachable only by phone. Now, he'd be answerable to messages and requests from colleagues no matter his whereabouts, no matter the hour. The Blackberry, and the concept of constant communication, had sparked a debate within the corporate world: Should employees be electronically tethered to management 24/7? Well, we know who won that argument in the end. The new tech was a blessing and a curse that fit neatly into the palm of his hand.

Often, he'd start his mornings at the office by spending the first few minutes at his desk scanning the old-fashioned newspaper headlines over coffee—*The Times* of London usually. One winter morning in January 2005, just a few months after his daughter was born, he was sad to read that Johnny Carson had passed away.

Johnny had never quit smoking and had died of emphysema.

"Those damn cigarettes," he'd said to his brother, shortly before his death.

SWITZERLAND CONFIDENTIAL

In June 2005, after about four years of working for the company, he was offered something new.

Switzerland had transformed into a hub for Western European and American businesses, and most of the company's regional teams in Europe, the Middle East, and Africa had already moved there, so it was a natural step for him. By continuing to work in the UK from the London office, he'd become the odd one out.

It wasn't surprising when, one morning at HQ, the order came down from above.

He was divested of responsibility for Central Asia and divested of Grand Prix and all other UK market assignments. In return, he was handed the files for France, Belgium, Luxembourg, and the Netherlands, in addition to the files he already held: Iberia and Italy. This meant he was now managing markets for all of Western Europe, with the exception of Germany. He was also given the Switzerland file and told it would be best if he moved there—to Lausanne.

The move was presented to him as a choice, not an order, but it was not the kind of request he could say no to. He knew he wouldn't be asked a second time.

That evening, he conferred with his wife.

She was hesitant, and for good reason. They now had their first child. They'd recently renovated their house. And the UK was where her family lived. To counter her fears, he presented her with the details of the package the company was offering.

The company would essentially pay for almost everything, other than their groceries. It would cover all accommodation costs, school fees, the cost of a nanny, and it would provide a car. It was also offering a massive bump in salary.

In theory, Switzerland was a much more expensive place to live, so the company was equalizing his salary from one market to another to adjust for the higher cost of, say, food and laundry detergent. It was basically giving him a 20 percent raise for the inconvenience of moving abroad to a more expensive place (this was back when an expat salary was still common). What the lawyer and his wife were being offered was, by any standard, exceptionally generous.

He would be making a tremendous amount of money, and the family would be paying for almost nothing on a daily, weekly, or monthly basis. His salary became pocket money, and family savings. He calculated that they could save $10,000 a month.

When he finished presenting his wife the package details, she said this to him: "Where do we sign?"

Most people think of Geneva when they hear Switzerland — probably because of the Geneva Convention — but he was being sent about thirty minutes outside of Geneva, to Lausanne.

Lausanne was famous for three things: a business school called the International Institute for Management Development; an international hotel and hospitality school called the École hôtelière de

Lausanne; and the International Olympic Committee (IOC). It's the seat of the Olympic Games, so there were always international delegations cruising around town in SUVs branded with those Olympic rings.

At the Olympic Museum and IOC headquarters, a rise of beautiful stone steps led up to the building's sleekly designed stone and glass facade—and on those steps was engraved the name of every city to play host over the history of the games. This was a monument to international athleticism, to human physical prowess.

For a city renowned for its dedication to cuisine, management skills, and sport, perhaps it wasn't a surprise, then, that Lausanne's lesser-known fourth claim to fame—as the tobacco capital of the world—was underplayed.

Lausanne was the home of Philip Morris International, the largest tobacco company of all tobacco companies in the world, excluding China. Philip Morris International was also the first big tobacco company to have made the move to Switzerland, and most tobacco companies followed its lead.

In a way, that's why he was relocating here. Twenty years earlier, an executive at Philip Morris had figured out they could make more money and, more importantly, be provided a safe haven from the threat of US lawsuits, if the company moved shop from New York State to Switzerland. Follow the leader.

Lausanne was relatively small, with a population of 140,000 people. Like most Swiss cities, it was spotless and manicured, and it was a global capital of luxury. All the major brands were here, including Louis Vuitton, Hermès, and the elite watch manufacturers Patek Philippe, Omega, and Jaeger-LeCoultre. It was a handsome city, and an expensive one in which to live.

The lawyer's home for the first number of weeks became the Lausanne Palace hotel, where his family lived while they hunted for an apartment and then waited for their furniture to arrive from the

UK. He became quite fond of the Palace, which housed an immaculate spa and fitness club, beautiful pool, a Michelin-starred restaurant, and breathtaking views of Lake Geneva.

Just down the street was the Beau-Rivage Palace. These were two of the most extraordinary and most expensive hotels in the world. They were grand, and both conveyed a quiet, modest authority in that perfectly Swiss manner. Dressed up, but not to attract attention or to show off. Old-world style.

After their short stint at the Lausanne Palace, they moved into a newly refurbished penthouse apartment that cost about $10,000 a month, with five bedrooms, a new kitchen, dining room, and a one-hundred-square-metre terrace with a stunning 180-degree view of Lake Geneva.

Across that sparkling lake was the French town of Évian, and the view they enjoyed from their terrace each morning was the image depicted on every bottle of Evian water: those three iconic mountains. The water coming out of their taps tasted like Evian. Basically, they now inhabited a beautiful commercial for better living.

They also had their own laundry room. Anywhere in Europe, having a laundry room in your apartment was a luxury, and early on this got them into trouble—albeit Swiss trouble. The floor in the laundry room was stone tile, so walking on it in shoes, having a baby run around in there, or simply putting on a load of laundry made some noise—enough noise to annoy the neighbours below them. The complaints came swiftly and were numerous. The concierge was rude to them and told them to be quiet.

In the lawyer's first week in the new apartment, the company's local lawyer, who was also a Swiss judge, took him out to welcome him to Lausanne.

Over lunch, the judge asked how his family was settling in.

The lawyer explained the details of the noise complaints and the exchange with the rude concierge.

The judge asked for the concierge's telephone number. Later that same evening, the concierge came to the lawyer's door to personally apologize.

When the lawyer saw the judge again, he told him about the apology.

"What did you tell him?" asked the lawyer.

"I'm not going to tell you everything we discussed, but I did say you were an important person to have in Switzerland for the economy."

He never asked for any more details, and from then on the concierge was extremely polite to his family.

Switzerland was a country famous for its rules, and those rules were not meant to be broken. This wasn't Rome or New York.

Rules were put in place for everyone's comfort and safety, and the letter and spirit of those rules were adhered to at all times. When social attitudes themselves failed to keep everything in check, there were police officers to enforce the rules. The wealth of the country meant it kept a very well-funded and attentive police force.

In Lausanne, if you called the police to complain about "noise pollution" after 10 P.M. — which was an offence — the police arrived at your door within minutes.

There's a famous story of two Swiss neighbours who decided to throw a party together. One neighbour went home at 11 P.M. and found the noise from the party he had helped organize irritating, so he called the police. The police showed up and shut down the party. The lawyer heard that this was a true story, but who knew. File under Swiss Urban Legend.

Here were a few rules his family had to learn, or were forced to comply with. His apartment rental contract specifically forbade him from urinating standing up after 10 P.M. This may sound crazy, but there was a reason behind the rule: noise pollution. Laundry on Sunday was similarly a no-go. This was because of the noise that the water travelling through the pipes might make, as well as the shaking of the machine, and the impact of that shaking on the building. Taking a shower at a certain time of night, or very early in the morning, was frowned upon too. Throwing the wrong piece of garbage in the wrong bin could bring you a heavy fine. Even keeping pets, such as fish, in singles rather than in pairs was an offence: it was considered cruel to the animals to make them live on their own.

They learned very quickly what the rules were, by trial and error, and they learned to comply or face the consequences: a dirty look from a neighbour, or a talking-to from the concierge. In Switzerland, people were always watching, and this meant everyone went about their days quietly, efficiently, politely.

The fascinating thing was that everybody did comply. After 10 P.M. at night, it really was quiet in the building, and presumably across the entire country.

It was the antithesis of the American "we're always open" culture.

The downside to all this was a certain social frigidity. People weren't rude, but they were distant. Most people they met were uninterested in taking any time to get to know them. People seemed to believe in keeping to themselves. The social culture lived up to the country's international stance: it was neutral. Which could be good or bad, depending on whether you wanted to make new friends or be left alone. They did figure out that they didn't need to lock their door at night, and no one ever parked in his parking spot at work—not once.

The lawyer felt he could have left a bag of money outside their door and somebody would ring the bell to inform them a bag of money had been left outside their door.

This sense of calm and order also meant there was no sense of immediacy to anything or anyone. The concept of getting something done fast did not exist—so no offer of free pizza if it wasn't delivered in half an hour. However, when a workman gave you an appointment for next Thursday at 10:15 A.M., he knocked on your door at 10:15 A.M. — always.

The trains really did run on time, to the second. The lawyer never witnessed, during all his time in Switzerland, a train that was late to leave a station. Shops closed for lunch and at the end of the day at 6 P.M. sharp, every day. And Saturday had restricted shopping hours.

Absolutely nothing was open on Sundays. This was a part of following the rules: you didn't work on Sunday; you went to church. And if you didn't happen to be a member of a church, you spent the day thoughtfully, quietly, with your family.

The incredible truth was that his family's quality of life quickly improved. The rules, it turned out, worked. Life really was better when shops were closed on Sundays. He spent more time with his wife and kids. He had more money to spend; he was away from corporate headquarters; he had an office three times the size of his old one; and he did less travelling. He could also go home for lunch if he wanted to.

It was civilized, and pleasant.

And although it did take them awhile, they eventually made friends. Mostly with other expats who had children, peers who were working for corporate entities like Philip Morris, Honeywell, Nestlé, Cadbury Schweppes, Honda, Nespresso, Starbucks, and Tetra Pak, the world's largest packaging company. Other companies with a footprint in Lausanne: Merck, for example, in pharmaceuticals; Monsanto in agrochemicals. Then throw in all the Swiss corporations, banks, chocolate companies, and watchmakers. Switzerland really did have the best chocolate in the world, which was strange, considering that never had an ounce of coco been grown or harvested there.

The lawyer was given a BMW X3, gunmetal grey, which he used to cruise around the country on weekends. He remembered fondly his first day of work for the company, that first company car being dropped off at his house in London and him cruising out of the city against the traffic to the office.

They also hired a nanny. In the interview, she told them her previous employer had been the Saudi royal family, and she explained she was looking for a more normal lifestyle.

Why had big tobacco companies set up international headquarters in Switzerland?

It wasn't for the chocolate, the watches, or for the bucolic setting. It wasn't because of the quiet evenings, nor was it because the trains ran on time. These were just bonuses.

There were two major reasons why the industry migrated to the Swiss mountains: to legally ring-fence their business against the possible threat of legal assault, and for the low corporate tax rate. These two issues were interlinked, like rings on the Olympic logo.

To understand what the lawyer was doing in Switzerland, let's go back to the surgeon general's report of 1964 and the beginning of that anti-tobacco wave.

By 1964, as you're aware, the American tobacco industry was at the very core of global popular culture. Smoking was cool; everybody did it.

Wait, let's go back further to World War II.

The eventual participation of the United States in the Second World War brought to Europe millions of American soldiers, and with them came what were now perceived as classic American brands: Coca-Cola, Hershey's chocolate, Campbell's soup, and American cigarettes.

Smoking was everywhere: on the battlefields and behind the front lines, and all through the military hierarchy. The movie stars they watched in cinemas smoked, and the music stars who entertained them smoked. Smoking was glamorous and aspirational, and a nice way to steal a break from the horror, or to kill time waiting for the battle. Lucky Strike, Kent, Pall Mall, Camel, Winston, Chesterfield, all of those American brands that had been invented in the American South were spreading across Europe along with the soldiers pushing back the Germans. Hitler, as you may recall, was not a smoker and was fervently anti-tobacco.

These American brands became synonymous with what was hopeful about the idea of America in the world: freedom and victory. American soldiers were smoking American brands across Europe, and they were heroes. The Old World admired that New World mythology and wanted the brands that represented it.

The war helped the American tobacco industry conquer Europe, and it was now the mission of those companies to secure and expand those foreign markets. These were his files now: Western Europe.

War was the origin of the European and then the global demand for American and Western brands, and that demand continued to this day. North Korea's Kim Jong-il may have threatened to destroy America, but he openly smoked Marlboro cigarettes.

Lucky Strike and Camel quickly became iconic brands in Europe, and this grew into an export market for American cigarette companies. And then it became something bigger.

Fast-forward a couple of decades, and throw in the implications of the 1964 surgeon general's report, when the domestic market in the US saw an immediate downturn in smoking and the threat of massive litigation.

In the 1970s, after the Ford Pinto case but before the security of the Master Settlement Agreement, the US judicial system trended towards the punitive damage system, and the tobacco industry was terrified. The business had grown—and it wasn't just American now, it was global. If a case went to court in the US and the jury ruled a certain way, it could wipe out the entire global industry, because the companies were based in the US.

Maybe this was the right time to come up with a contingency plan—perhaps buy a second home.

So Philip Morris decided to secure the ownership of their valuable brands somewhere outside of the US. That way, if any legal case in the US went sideways, the company would still be able to rely on those international markets that had matured since the war and operate that growing portion of the business from a safe place outside the US.

Switzerland became the most attractive option for a second home, because the Swiss government worked diligently to make it attractive.

There is a reason why most US companies didn't suddenly relocate to an economically kinder international base: money.

A multi-billion-dollar US company that possessed the most valuable brand recognition in the world couldn't just say goodbye to America and sail away. Leaving the US was a very expensive move to contemplate, because the American government—specifically the IRS—wouldn't just let you operate in the US for decades, make billions of dollars, and then walk out the door without giving you a hard slap in the face.

The slap in the face was called an exit charge.

Philip Morris was, of course, famously a Southern US tobacco company, based in Richmond, Virginia. Their postwar success with the Marlboro brand propelled it to global success, and also brought several ownership changes, with large corporations such as Kraft Foods and then Altria, owning controlling shares.

The value in that business was held in the US, because the American company owned the international trademarks to Marlboro, Chesterfield, and many other profitable brands sold in the domestic market there and also, more importantly, across the world.

The brilliant solution Philip Morris came up with wasn't to relocate. Instead, it decided to "spin off" its international business from its US company, and this meant creating a new company called Philip Morris International (PMI).

Once PMI was created, Philip Morris, the US company, would willingly sell it its international trademarks.

The US corporation and the newly formed PMI would be the same company in name only; legally, they would have nothing to do with each other. It was like making a clone of yourself and then sending that clone to live in a completely different part of the world while you stayed at home and never even exchanging a postcard.

This new arrangement was of great interest to the IRS, which regarded the manoeuvre as fleeing from the US. The transaction between the two companies was seen as a "capital gain event." The IRS taxed Philip Morris the full value of the capital gain that would have been achieved had those international trademarks (Marlboro among them) been sold at full market value to a competitor, for a profit.

For the IRS, it was as if Philip Morris was selling all its brands to another international player to profit from in all those lucrative international markets. This transaction could be worth billions of US dollars.

Still, no matter the hit from the IRS, there was the threat of a legal case that could vaporize the US company if it did nothing. Wouldn't you pay a fortune to live another day? Philip Morris set up its new international headquarters in Lausanne, and it paid dearly for it.

The transaction eventually created two completely independent companies with shared brands, and at the same time successfully contained American legal liability to include only those assets owned by the US company, should the worst-case scenario actually come to be—a legal decision that bankrupted the US tobacco industry.

All other major tobacco companies watched what Philip Morris was doing and soon found their own ways to follow them to Switzerland.

So here he was, cruising around Lausanne in the gunmetal Beemer.

He'd often pass the HQ of PMI, a compound in the heart of the city with tiered, brutalist-style, low-built buildings. There was nothing opulent about the design; you'd never know it was the epicentre of the mighty Marlboro global empire. The lawyer never did get an invitation into that office.

And right next door was the other tobacco giant: British American Tobacco, or BAT for short.

Also ranked as one of the world's largest corporations, BAT had opened their European headquarters in Lausanne just after PMI and continued to operate many of their European business lines from there.

Unlike Philip Morris, however, BAT still hadn't taken the leap of moving their entire international business and ownership to Switzerland, largely because they had always been a British company and had not faced the same legal problems Philip Morris did in the US; there was no equivalent of the Master Settlement Agreement in the UK. Instead, at first there were voluntary agreements, followed by those European Union directives the lawyer had spent so much time on and practically memorized.

So BAT had never had to endure the financial pain of an exit charge from the UK by triggering a capital gain event, and had not sold their trademarks to an international version of its company in Switzerland. The option was always there for BAT, though, just in case. Never say never. Their office in Lausanne was essentially one big parachute the company could deploy in case of emergency.

The lawyer and his colleagues were always particularly nice to any BAT employees they might encounter in Lausanne. Why?

It went back to those early days of circling London with the drive teams. If you didn't have the power to recruit new smokers, all you could do was fight to keep the business of current smokers—with deals and marketing tradecraft, hoping to lure them to your company's brands. Consolidation was just a bigger move in this strategy, buying an entire company, its brands, and therefore its smokers. This was the trend in the industry.

In his opinion, it wasn't a question of whether the lawyer's company was going to be taken over; it was a question of who was going to buy it, and when.

And the most likely candidate to take over his company was BAT, because they were rich, and because they were British.

It wasn't as if he knew anything definitive from a corporate or strategic standpoint, but BAT was a fellow UK-traded tobacco company; it was larger than his company; and it had more cash. What was more, some of their brand ownership crossed over in global markets; their flagship brands in Europe were owned in some other parts of the world by BAT.

BAT was also a likely match because even though they were a global British tobacco company, in his opinion they had a bullshit business in their home market compared to his own company. If BAT bought his company, it could cement their place not just around the world but at home in Britain too.

So, he and his colleagues lived in fear of the big BAT coming in swinging. As an inside joke, they called them "the evil empire."

The lawyer couldn't recall a month that went by where the spectre of BAT wasn't discussed in his department. As a result, he was always very respectful and accommodating when dealing with BAT staff and management. One day, they could be his colleagues and his bosses.

———

Everyone was here in this beautiful Swiss setting because of Philip Morris. But just to be clear, who had paid for their move?

The government of Switzerland had paid for it—in a way.

One of the advantages for a major company moving their head office to Switzerland was that it was possible to sit down with the Swiss authorities and negotiate a tax rate. So, for example, it could be possible for a company that was incurring a massive exit charge to negotiate a deal with the Swiss that stated it would not pay taxes for the first five years the company did business there. Sounds good, right?

Legend had it that when Philip Morris executives sat down with Swiss representatives, they were offered a deal that was impossible to refuse. That deal was still being gossiped about in industry circles: set up shop here, and don't pay corporate taxes for twenty years—as legend had it.

You may be asking yourself why Switzerland would offer such a ridiculous deal. How was it worth it to provide safe harbour to one of the most contentious and profitable international companies in the history of consumer products without it paying a corporate tax bill for twenty years?

First of all, the Swiss took a long-term view. If you've ever strolled through Lausanne or Basel, you've seen their medieval city centres. This was a very old culture; twenty years was nothing. After all, they'd been brokering international business deals for over a thousand years.

Second, the authorities took a broad view of the benefits of having thousands of employees spending their money and using services in Switzerland. The families of these executives would send their children to international schools, dine at the finest restaurants—and they would pay tax on all those services.

And with Lausanne being a small city, a thousand new employees meant something—particularly at the upper echelon of the economic service sector. And look at what the result had achieved: a leader made a move, and the entire industry followed.

It turned out to be the perfect haven for an international tobacco company.

Just look at what was valued by the Swiss.

Neutrality, for example.

Not many countries in the world were officially a neutral state. This meant, of course, that during World War II, the Germans, the French, the Russians, and whoever else wanted to could haul their treasures and riches to Switzerland for safekeeping. Win or lose, your wealth would be protected by a Swiss banking company. This meant, as well, that many Jewish families showed up at the border and were turned away. Neutrality had its price. It wasn't an evaluation based on one event or another; it was an enshrined legal position in this nation.

Banking confidentiality was also valued, and enshrined in Swiss law as well, the way freedom of speech was in America. It was a matter of national pride. The concept of confidentiality was a core belief, and that attitude also applied more broadly to a discreet and non-judgmental approach when it came to the business in which an individual might be working.

The lawyer wasn't sure if a lot of arms dealers were located in Switzerland, but it wouldn't have surprised him at all. It was a good place to be if what you were selling wasn't socially popular but was profitable, and if you were willing to follow the rules.

For a multinational tobacco company under fire from almost every corner of the world for damaging the health of people in every country, every day of every year, one could easily see the benefit of operating out of such an environment. As long as a person, or a company, was invited to stay and was following the rules, they were treated with dignity and respect.

"Business as usual" was the vibe here, and business was very good. And another bonus: the Swiss were also, generally speaking, still fans of smoking.

In Switzerland the lawyer arrived to a noticeably European country that was distinctly outside of the European Union. They didn't use the euro but the Swiss franc.

Happily, the regulations and directives of the EU did not apply in Switzerland.

After he arrived, though, changes to the local market seemed to be afoot, with more regulations looming; the Surgeon General's Warning seemed to be following him as he moved. And yet, as if by magic, those regulations sweeping across much of Europe never materialized here.

It wasn't magic, though; it was influence.

Up the street, so to speak—in Geneva—was the home of the World Health Organization, dedicated to championing a healthy future for all citizens of the world, which had sprouted from the United Nations initiative.

Back in 2003, the WHO had created its own anti-tobacco treatise, the Framework Convention on Tobacco Control. This was a playbook for all countries to follow, in order to help manage what the WHO identified as a global health epidemic. Over one hundred countries signed on, including Switzerland.

Yet unlike all the members of the European Union—and in a twist of irony—the Swiss government didn't ratify the agreement. The made-in-Switzerland framework had been the guiding force propelling those EU directives which the lawyer had spent so much time poring over. Of course, Switzerland had decided to remain outside the EU—and while the WHO's tobacco framework was being hammered together in Geneva, the largest and wealthiest tobacco companies in the world had quietly moved into this

country and made it their home. The lets-sign-but-not-ratify government position on the WHO framework was perhaps yet another
example of the constant tension built into Swiss neutrality.

For now, his company continued making a lot of money here.
Advertising remained mostly legal, with no draconian health warnings yet either. A smoker could pretty much smoke wherever they
wanted. Those anti-smoking waves seemed to break on those Swiss
mountain ranges.

The lawyer was now counsel for most Western European business, and responsible for legal affairs and all their related companies, together with the duty-free business as well as a European joint
venture with R.J. Reynolds Tobacco.

He sat on the boards of all the operating companies, which meant
more contractual work, advertising clearances, and general commercial duties, and it involved travel to some of the most beautiful
cities in the world: Rome, Lisbon, Paris, Brussels, and his old favourite, Madrid.

It was a relief. The lawyer was working in a senior position without being in a corporate headquarters. He put his suits away in a
closet and could wear business casual to the office. This may sound
like a small perk, but it was major; he now lived in the comfort
zone. Once, on a really hot day when most people were on summer
vacation, he crossed the line and wore shorts and a T-shirt. The president of the Swiss office spotted him, though, and sent him home
to change. Still, the prez was very polite about the whole thing.

Another perk at the new office: Google search capability. At HQ
in London, his internet access had been blocked, but here he could
surf the net freely and increasingly read his favourite newspapers
online, all while sporting a more comfortable office uniform.

He became friendly with the executives. And their Swiss operation was exceeding financial expectations. The international company was delivering good news and a pipeline of profits back to the

home team in London. They sailed onward on these international waters, this little ship of business-casual pirates.

In Western Europe and in North America, the waves of the surgeon general's report were dousing the flames of the industry. Here, though, with the Evian view and the quiet precision of Swiss business culture ticking along, the company was thriving and international business was growing—thanks to Kazakhstan and so many other global frontiers. This was the good life.

Of course, it couldn't last—because, as everyone knows, the good times just don't.

THE BIGGER FISH

Most smokers believed that the most popular cigarette in the world was Marlboro—and that was true.

Marlboro was the most popular cigarette brand in the western hemisphere. But when you took the astronaut's perspective and looked down at the big blue marble from space, the most popular cigarette in the eastern hemisphere was not a Western brand at all; it was a series of Asian brands. In Japan, for example, the reigning cigarette was called Mild Seven, manufactured by Japan Tobacco, a company that had set up an international office just up the road in Geneva.

Fact: the government of Japan owned 50 percent of the largest tobacco company in Japan, which made one of the most sought-after cigarettes on the planet, but most Westerners had probably never heard of Mild Seven or Japan Tobacco.

Why would a government own a major share of a tobacco company? It seems outrageous, given the current social climate.

Up until the mid-1980s, the tobacco business was profitable and generally socially palatable. While regulating this contentious yet popular product, many governments wanted to continue to benefit from those valuable, if also now perceived as evil, empires.

One way to profit was to tax the product, of course, but many countries owned slices of their tobacco trade, if not the entire pie. It may have been counterintuitive, but it was business as usual in a surprising number of nations, including Japan and China.

Remember, Spain's once enormous global empire was generally considered to be the first tobacco monopoly in history, but other colonial empires of the era emulated the monopoly model, most notably France, Portugal, and Austria. Years later, China did so as well.

In fact, China, currently the world's most populous country, was also its largest manufacturer of cigarettes—and by far. Some estimates put China's cigarette production at 40 percent of the global market. But no one in the West really worried about Chinese cigarette expansion, because the company that produced them was state owned, and it didn't seem to care about conquering foreign markets. So there was a quiet truce in that arena.

Basically, China's message was as follows: "We'll make cigarettes for our population of over 1.4 billion people—with an estimated three hundred million smokers—and we won't bother you. But please don't bother us. Thank you. That is all."

In China, there was one state-owned company that supplied all brands of cigarettes—sort of like in the Canary Islands, only a lot bigger. And if a Western company wanted access to even a small share of that gargantuan market, they had to partner with China Tobacco.

Thailand, Vietnam, Iran, Iraq, Syria, Lebanon, and Tunisia: all of these countries currently owned tobacco companies. And many more nations had big slices of the trade. The government of India—which managed the second-largest population on Earth at 1.39 billion people—owned about a quarter of the tobacco company ITC, originally an initialism for India Tobacco Company.

So government investment or ownership in tobacco wasn't unusual—it just felt like it should be, given the waves of anti-tobacco sentiment sweeping the globe.

Why did governments continue to invest in tobacco products? If you remember, the Canary Islands had laws to ensure cigarettes were manufactured locally, giving the resident population jobs and keeping out foreign-made products. And you recall the attitude in Spain towards foreign product, except in Fake Spain: "Go fuck yourself."

In Japan Tobacco's case, they were a massive player in Asia that had managed to hold Western cigarette brands at bay in their island nation. But they had not ventured to push their influence into Western markets, until they pulled a surprising move.

When the lawyer drove from Lausanne to Geneva, he'd spy the home of R.J. Reynolds Tobacco International (RJR), which was historically based in Winston-Salem, North Carolina, and which had also achieved global success with iconic American cigarette brands such as Winston, Camel, his beloved Vantage, and more recently Natural American Spirit.

RJR's international business had also grown steadily in the postwar era, and it too was attracted to Switzerland as a base for its international business outside of the United States. RJR followed the leader, choosing Switzerland for tax reasons.

Much like Philip Morris, RJR went through some ownership changes over the years (when it merged with Nabisco, for example; read *Barbarians at the Gate* if you want the salacious details), and ran into some financial trouble in the US in the late 1990s as the Master Settlement Agreement was being hammered out.

As a way to raise some serious cash fast, RJR put its international business—RJR International, which consisted of all business outside of the US and Puerto Rico—up for sale.

Everyone assumed that Philip Morris International or the lawyer's company would snap it up. But in a surprise move, its iconic Western brands were acquired for billions of dollars by Japan Tobacco. Japan Tobacco outbid Philip Morris and the lawyer's company by over one billion dollars.

Rumour had it the Japanese raised the bid by one billion dollars because it was a round number that RJR would be unable to refuse. It was a *Godfather*-style offer; no company could turn away from an extra billion dollars.

Ultimately, the deal created Japan Tobacco International, based in Geneva. Consolidation was expensive, but among the benefits were the Geneva RJR employees and their office, already up and running.

Overnight, the deal supersized Japan Tobacco into a global player. Now his company and Philip Morris were watching them closely, because they obviously had a hunger to expand their Western market share.

In a way, the Japanese company was doing now what the Americans had set out to accomplish decades earlier: searching out brave new markets across the ocean from their home base. The Japanese government was buying all those iconic American brands that had matured during World War II. They were the new pirates, sailing into the fray from the East.

And then it happened, shortly before the December 2006 holidays.

A deal was struck behind closed doors, hands were shaken, signatures were applied, and suddenly the lawyer was working for Japan Tobacco.

The deal was done, subject to the regulatory red tape you'd get with any kind of international takeover.

The lawyer found out about the massive transaction on the day the public found out about it; the $18-billion deal was big news, announced in business news dailies around the world.

It was at the time the largest foreign takeover in history by a Japanese company, and it was for dried leaves and paper. The deal was titanic: billions of dollars for a cigarette company, post Surgeon General's Warning, while the global industry was under intense attack.

Most of his colleagues were not happy at the news, and everyone was fearful about losing their jobs.

It turned out to be a rational fear.

Once the takeover was announced, there was a regulatory closing period of three or four months. They were told to continue doing their jobs as normal—"keep calm and carry on"—and act as if the takeover had not happened.

Over that time, in that corporate limbo, the lawyer did very little. No one really knew what to do; everyone just tried to keep quiet and pray that their paychecks would be deposited.

As with any corporate takeover of this gargantuan nature, it was common that the top tier of management would immediately be axed, while the lower-downs of the company were integrated. The big fish ate the medium-sized fish but allowed the minnows to swim along. He wasn't sure which tier he belonged to.

His boss and his boss's boss were let go with lucrative exit packages. Mary, who had been his protector for years but had ascended to several rungs above him, left the company almost immediately after the deal was closed. Her boss, as well as the president of the Swiss office, soon followed.

As a general rule, Japan Tobacco was extremely generous and utterly professional in the way it took over the company. Its management of the transition was courteous in every aspect of business etiquette.

He did not hear one unhappy story about how things were handled after the takeover. So he watched a quiet parade of people he'd known, admired, and worked with exit the company. Goodbye. So great to work with you. Good luck.

He waited for his own execution, and then waited some more. But he wasn't handed a pink slip, which was confusing. He sat and twiddled his thumbs for weeks, watching for news of his fate.

On the day the transaction finally closed officially, the lawyer received a phone call from the general counsel of Japan Tobacco International (JTI) and was invited to attend a meeting at the office in Geneva, a half-hour drive from where he lived.

His instructions included which building to go to and where to park. He followed his instructions.

At home, he literally dusted off his suit, which he hadn't had to wear for the past two years, and he polished his shoes. He knew that JTI adhered to a strict Japanese business policy of formal attire. He also polished up his resumé and printed out a few copies. That night, he slept poorly.

In the morning, he got into his BMW, pressed his polished shoe to the pedal, and sped to Geneva along the perfectly smooth Swiss asphalt. He felt as if he were racing to the end of Tobacco Road.

His meeting at JTI was with human resources staff only.

He sat down and was offered a drink and then, without much introduction or time spent on formalities, was told that JTI wanted to keep him on as a lawyer with the company and that he was being offered the role of assistant general counsel, director. He was informed that this was a position looking after legal business development.

The offer was a shock. He tried to keep a poker face. He'd had very little experience in the area in which he was being offered work.

Then a contract was pushed under his nose with a salary figure on it that made his eyes pop. He really couldn't believe the number he was looking at.

HR informed him he had one week to make up his mind. The number made up his mind, but he had to clear it with his teammate.

He went home and discussed the offer with his wife. She was also confused. They were both extremely pleased, though, at the salary he was being offered. He'd been making a huge amount of money, but now they could afford to buy property anywhere in the world. He thought about the Canary Islands and those fresh sliced pineapples and the heavenly weather all year round.

In the morning, he sent an email to the general counsel of JTI informing them that that he was delighted to be considered. They haggled a little, and in the end he accepted the role. He was now earning more than half a million dollars a year, and he was thirty-four years old.

Even more of a shock: out of all the highly qualified employees who worked in the Swiss office, he was the only one who survived the takeover. Every other executive pirate was sent to walk the plank, while he was ordered to get back to work on deck.

He watched each colleague drop away into the stormy international waters of consolidation, until no familiar face was left on his ship, which now sailed under a new flag.

This new crew was different.

The lawyer didn't know them, and the amount JTI was paying him made him suspicious. He also wondered why the company had given him a role in an area in which he had very little experience. He was suspicious generally. This was his state of mind.

As if to counter this skepticism, the new legal team turned out to be pretty much without exception made up of really nice people, all of whom were European or American. They weren't as warm as his colleagues in Madrid, but they were kind and respectful.

He was determined not to let down his guard, though. This was a massive change for him, moving from a successful outpost of a British company with so much freedom back to a strict corporate culture. It was a golden handcuffs kind of situation: show up early, tie pressed, and stay late and earn that massive salary. It didn't really get more corporate.

Eventually, he did gain some clarity as to why he was spared the plank. It turned out his name had been on an infamous internal list of managers that was penned in the frantic final hours of the takeover by a few executives at the old company—a list of who should be spared for their valued knowledge. At least that mystery was solved.

Oddly, he was now tasked with dismantling parts of his previous employer's empire. This new role turned out to be a white-collar version of selling off parts of an old truck: the Department of Business Anti-Development.

His suspiciousness came and went, but the mirror structure didn't help.

He came to learn that each senior Western-facing employee had a Japanese counterpart—a mirror employee in the Tokyo office. This meant there were certain Japanese men who attended meetings with him—silently. They were shadows, who observed and reported everything discussed back to executives at the Tokyo headquarters. It was odd, adding more absurdity to the already bizarre professional situation.

The other thing that got to him was the formality. The way everyone dressed. The old-fashioned way in which people required you to act in accordance with your level at the company. It was old school, even for Switzerland—which was saying a lot.

As an example, his security pass allowed him access only to certain floors based on his level of seniority. He was unable to walk up to the board level to discuss something with his superiors. He had no desire to go up there, but it did present a problem when he was invited to meetings upstairs and the damn pass didn't work.

It reminded him a lot of his first days as a junior lawyer during inductions. Everything seemed new again, and strange.

One Friday, a senior director requested that the lawyer put together some legal papers for a business transaction. He would need to work the entire weekend on those documents, and he did. On Monday, he arrived at the office at 5 A.M. in order to proofread his work. He did so, and went to his manager's office at 8:30 A.M. with proofed documents in hand to take him through the details.

The director looked at him and asked this question.

"Where's your tie?"

"It's downstairs at my desk," the bleary-eyed lawyer answered.

The superior looked him straight in the eye.

"When you put on your tie, we can talk about the agreement."

This was not an isolated incident.

The workload was heavy, but he managed.

For the first time in his professional career, however, he felt vulnerable and helpless in terms of what he was doing, despite the fact that he was a qualified and experienced lawyer. And he didn't have a protector anymore, either; six months had dragged by since his former dream team had walked the plank.

He was very pleased one day, then, to see in the dining room his former CEO having lunch. Let's call him Giles.

Giles had been axed but had agreed to stay on for a short period following the takeover to assist with the transition. He told the lawyer he was going to be in Geneva for a couple of months, and it would be nice to have a drink sometime.

Later that afternoon, the lawyer managed to find out where in the building the former CEO's office was located. He found Giles in his office with the former finance director and was invited in for a smoke and a chat.

They all had a good laugh about the shock of the takeover and the many changes taking place. They asked him how he was getting on, and how his family was.

After having a decent chat, Giles looked at the lawyer and made a prediction.

"You know, I'm going to make a bet with you," he said. "I bet you won't last more than a year in this company."

The truth was, the lawyer knew he needed to find a way out. But the very process that had swallowed his company also made it a challenge to exit. Consolidation, on a global level, meant there were fewer alternatives out there.

In a way, this wasn't new. It was actually like going back in time, a return to the old order, when, towards the close of the nineteenth century, two fiery titans controlled much of the global industry: the American Tobacco Company and Britain's Imperial Tobacco. Those two entities briefly merged into the behemoth British American Tobacco Company with the ambition of global domination, swiftly setting up tobacco operations around the world, including in China and Japan.

The combined influence of this monster-sized British-American corporation—a perfect union of Old and New World powerhouses —was considered so influential, so powerful, that it was ruled to be monopoly that had cornered a lucrative market. So the joint venture was outlawed and broken up into smaller companies—including the big BAT. In fact, after the Chinese monarchy was overthrown in 1911, the new republic had also thwarted Western ambitions to rule the tobacco industry of that country.

Now, a century later, the entire industry seemed to be collapsing back into that historical consolidated model, as if pulled together by the mysterious forces of capitalism. And indeed, just a few months after Japan Tobacco had finalized its takeover of his company, Britain's Imperial Tobacco bought up the corporate descendent of those Spanish and French tobacco dynasties—Altadis—for $17 billion.

Consolidation seemed to be leading to a reformation—if slightly reconfigured—of just a few fiery titans ruling over global empires of sticks.

Meanwhile, his new role in business anti-development plodded on.

JTI was a cigarette manufacturer and marketing company, and it concentrated on selling a portfolio of global flagship brands, along with selected regional brands. The company was not interested in selling cigars or pipes. That was old man stuff.

That meant the lawyer spent the following year selling businesses and dismantling the ventures his team had worked so diligently to build. He oversaw the legal work for selling off some distribution businesses, and he sold some Cuban and Dominican tobacco trademarks and cigar factories.

Perspective: he was studying the numbers on the Dominican factory he was now charged with selling. That factory had three hundred employees, all making cigars. Putting together the information memorandum that third parties would see, one detail jumped out for him. He was examining the page listing all of the employees, and the total salary cost of every employee. When he added up the salaries of those three hundred employees, he realized he made more money than all of them combined. It was depressing—and he also felt incredibly lucky.

It seemed it was his fate, and his job, to take apart what he had built and to make all of it redundant, and he was being paid a small fortune to do it.

Then something even more absurd occurred.

After he had dismantled everything, the lawyer was promoted to president and chair of the board for the old British company's international operations . . . on paper. His sole function in the top role at the Swiss office was to shut it down.

It was the lawyer's signature as president that officially closed the British operation and transferred it to Japanese control. He was a paper king for a day, proclaiming the end of the kingdom. It was a sad ceremony—a beheading of sorts.

The king is dead, long live the king.

Heavy times.

There was a trip for the JTI staff to go to Japan, and a number of the lawyers were invited, but he was not included on the list.

This just added to his suspicion that the axe was coming.

He thought the writing was on the wall when his boss called him about a receipt for a taxi from the airport. He'd been taking flights that cost tens of thousands of dollars, and there was a complaint about a receipt for a taxi?

Then, instead, he received a salary increase. Nothing was making sense to him, and he couldn't read the situation.

He spent a lot of time complaining to his wife about the particularly lethal cultural collision of Japanese-style office politics and Swiss-style stuffiness. He was being paid a king's ransom but becoming a total grouch. And he couldn't see any real prospect of finding another job of this calibre in the industry.

The bright spot for him during those strange days was when his wife informed him that they would be welcoming a new child into their family. He was overjoyed, but the happy news made him only more anxious about figuring out his next professional move.

Then, out of the blue, on a visit to Switzerland, the president of R.J. Reynolds' international operations contacted the lawyer and asked for a meeting.

It was an intriguing request. RJR was, so far, one of a handful of powerful American companies that had resisted consolidation, and it was doing well; it was one of those grand old tobacco dynasties in the Southern US, and even though a big chunk of its global business had been bought by Japan, it still had a small, respectable international operation.

At the meeting, the president told him that the Legend was retiring and they were looking for a qualified lawyer to replace him —although they'd be tweaking the job description—and needed someone who could operate from their Zurich office as an expat.

Who was the Legend? He was a seasoned, Southern-based gentleman tobacco lawyer with a vast international network who had helped keep the US industry on course through stormy times, and now he was apparently sailing into the sunset.

The lawyer was asked to attend a meeting with the general counsel—let's call her Jane—of Reynolds American, the holding company that owned R.J. Reynolds Global Products.

Jane requested to meet with the lawyer in London, but not in an office. She suggested they meet at the hotel where she was staying. Okay—it was only slightly cloak and dagger. The lawyer flew to London, and Reynolds paid.

He went straight from Heathrow to Jane's hotel and asked for her at reception, but she hadn't arrived yet. The concierge escorted him to a suite in the hotel, which had a meeting room attached to it. There was a massive king-sized bed. He wondered who he would have to sleep with to get this job.

Jane was about twenty minutes late, so he just sat in the large room with the bed.

He made a mistake in lighting a cigarette, not realizing that the hotel had become non-smoking. Since he had moved to Switzerland, the act banning smoking in public places had taken effect.

It was when he went to put out his cigarette that he realized there was no ashtray—damn it. It was a long time since he'd been in a hotel in London.

Jane entered the room a few minutes later, smoke still lingering in the air.

Jane had that Northeastern US, Ivy League feel. They talked for more than two hours: about tobacco issues, about his experience in the industry, and about what the position was that RJR was seeking to create, since replacing the Legend was impossible.

He left the meeting feeling very positive, and it reminded him of how he'd felt—so long ago now, it seemed—meeting with Mary and Heather, the headhunter. Sure enough, by the time he landed back in Switzerland, an email was waiting in his inbox, stating that Reynolds would like to offer him the position.

A few days later, Reynolds's HR department in Winston-Salem got in touch, and to his delight they offered a generous salary, expat terms in which the company paid for schooling, airfare, everything. He had managed to secure an expat agreement without leaving the country. He was getting ready to board a new pirate ship.

After agreeing to terms with RJR, the company initiated quite a lengthy security procedure. Unlike his previous employers, who relied on his resumé for references, RJR checked everything: they verified all of his previous employment and all of his post-secondary qualifications. He had never experienced anything like it before, but he had nothing to hide, so he went along with it.

Then he signed a contract. The only step left for the lawyer to do now was to resign from JTI.

He went in to the JTI office and wrote a letter of resignation.

Then he went to his director's office, and the director started to talk to him about something. The lawyer paused the conversation and told his colleague that he was resigning.

The director nodded. "Okay," he said. "Thank you. I'll come talk to you later."

This was really eerie. It was as if the director had been expecting his resignation.

After about thirty minutes, the director appeared at the lawyer's door and asked him to leave the premises. Security checked his bag and pockets and relieved him of his mobile and security pass. And that was that.

A couple of days later, he received a letter asking him to sign a termination agreement. It contained the details of what they were going to pay him out. They calculated everything to his advantage; it was extremely generous. He'd handed in his notice and they'd given him half a million dollars for leaving. No strings attached, no arguments.

He was also invited to an exit interview, which he had never experienced before. After that interview, JTI contacted Reynolds to let them know he was privy to a lot of company information.

Under the terms of the termination agreement, he was required to go on "garden leave," which was a three-month period to stay home and do nothing. It was quite possibly the most enjoyable three months of his life—twelve weeks at home with his wife and two daughters. They travelled and spent quality time together.

His new employer, Reynolds, decided they wanted the lawyer to spend the first week of his new role in Winston-Salem, for inductions. They booked him to fly to Greensboro. The next morning, the lawyer got up early and flew to the heart of American tobacco country, and when he arrived for his official first day of work, in the summer of 2008, no one at Reynolds asked him for any travel receipts.

Thankfully, there was always a bigger fish.

AMERICAN SPIRITS

Two of the most popular cigarette brands in US history were named after a town in North Carolina: Winston-Salem.

This was the seat of the R.J. Reynolds tobacco empire. The local high school was RJR High. The baseball team, in a grammatically sly turn, was called the Winston-Salem Dash. Many of the streets here were named after the Reynolds family, including the one that ran through its centre: Reynolds Boulevard.

When Brown & Williamson, Lorillard, and R.J. Reynolds grew rich here in the glory days of smoking in the mid-1900s, this region of the country came to be known as Tobacco Road. The road would soon stretch across the entire United States, and then, as the lawyer had witnessed, across the continents of the world.

As the seat of a vast empire, Winston-Salem looked like a town that had had its day, and that day was long gone.

The downtown core had thinned out, with many storefronts and shops left empty, boarded up, covered in graffiti, or converted into pawn shops. Clearly, commerce had been moving out to the surrounding suburbs, a fate that urban theorist Jane Jacobs had prophesized for so many American cities, though there were big medical and academic communities left intact here. Reynolds was not the force it once was, and other iconic American companies, such as Sara Lee, had shuttered here—but it wasn't Detroit, yet.

The legacy of the town's former glory was imbedded in the details of its still-beautiful neighbourhoods, populated with spacious, wonderful colonial and pre-war homes. If you've ever seen *Dawson's Creek*, that is what it looked like.

The Reynolds headquarters, famous in architecture circles, was the prototype for the Empire State Building, though few tourists who visited its larger and more famous younger sibling in New York realized this edifice in Winston-Salem had been constructed as a smaller test run before the Empire State Building arose over the Manhattan skyline.

Yes, the mini version was stunning: an elegant art deco structure with ornate elevators and gorgeous spaces. The building was not created to house the modular offices that later became standard, so it grew increasingly difficult to use with the corporate trend towards cubicles.

In the 1980s, as the Reynolds company expanded and needed more space, it built the RJR Plaza Building right next door, designed for the standard new office set-up, and the two buildings were connected by a covered atrium. A pity that the company eventually vacated its beautiful art deco jewel, and now just used the Plaza.

Though the lawyer was still working out of Switzerland, he was given a second office here in the Southern US, at the Plaza.

After the slog of a transatlantic flight, the lawyer always enjoyed arriving at the Greensboro airport, where you could walk off the plane, get your bags, and be riding on ground transportation into town within five minutes. There was never any traffic. Without exception, everyone was warm and cheerful with him. Southern hospitality existed, and it had outlasted some of the empires it had helped create.

Winston-Salem had only a few good restaurants, and of those just a handful had tablecloths on their tables. But the good ones were excellent, serving up traditional Southern fare: barbecue and grilled steaks and chops. Oh, baby.

One of his favourite meals was breakfast at the hotel. He would order chicken fried steak with country gravy, fried eggs, hash browns, and bacon. And he'd wash it down with a glass of cold sweet tea. It always amused him that if he wanted hot tea here, he had to ask for "hot" tea.

Having lived in Europe for so many years, it was refreshing for him, a Canadian, to come home to North America and experience American convenience and culture. Open on Sunday; open twenty-four hours!

The weather in Winston-Salem was just like the attitude, always warm. Even in the winter, when he needed to wear a light coat, it was never really cold, and certainly never snowed. In the summer, when it was hot, it was *really* hot. We're talking Southern heat that wilts the soul.

It was this kind of heat that colonists, followed by enslaved labourers—the early generations of African Americans who had been violently transplanted here—and then American farmers had endured working the fields in the broiling sun, stooped over to pick the leaves, curing and drying them, to supply the global appetite of the industry.

Tobacco farming continued to be very much alive in North Carolina, and Reynolds still had a large tobacco factory open in the region, just a few miles away—in Tobaccoville, believe or not. When that factory had opened, in 1987, it was a state-of-the-art facility and was celebrated in the *New York Times*: "Each machine at the new \$1 billion factory can turn out 8,000 cigarettes a minute. By December, when the plant reaches full capacity with 72 machines, it will be able to produce 576,000 cigarettes a minute. That means 110 billion cigarettes a year, about 20 percent of the total annual output of the domestic tobacco industry."

Fred Flintstone used to smoke Winston cigarettes, and NBC had a nightly news show called *Camel News Caravan*—which aired right before Johnny Carson, by the way. The iconic *I Love Lucy* was originally sponsored by Philip Morris, and, wow, did Lucy and all of her friends smoke!

Tobacco Road was the birthplace of many iconic cigarette brands, beyond Winston and Salem, including Camel, Newport, Kent, Kool, Virginia Slims, Doral, Lucky Strike, and, yes, his personal favourite, Vantage.

The area was also the home, for a time, of Jeffrey Wigand, when he worked at Brown & Williamson as its head of research and development—before his famous appearance on *60 Minutes*.

Wigand's damning revelations on *60 Minutes* about his experience at Brown & Williamson, specifically about spiking nicotine levels in cigarettes, added momentum to the change begun by the surgeon general's 1964 report and helped spur the Master Settlement Agreement, that punishing $200-billion payout that was meant to hit the US industry when it was down. And really, when the term "industry" is used, we're talking about a trio of players. Big players, yes, but just three major tobacco companies were left in the US as consolidation continued to play out.

It was an intimate gathering: Philip Morris, based nearby in Virginia; Reynolds American, based in Winston-Salem; and the one-hit-wonder Lorillard, in Greensboro, which was pretty much a one-brand company. Lorillard's Newport brand remains the best-selling menthol cigarette in the US—and to be fair, it's an incredible cigarette.

These three giants controlled the bulk of the tobacco market in America—all of the glory, including those supersized profits, but all of the ire and pain too.

By the time the lawyer started at Reynolds—in the summer of 2008—one iconic Southern cigarette brand was even experiencing a surprising renaissance on American televisions, in spite of the advertising ban, thanks to AMC's *Mad Men*. That stylish and groundbreaking series had premiered a year earlier, and it chronicled a fictitious advertising agency in the early 1960s, along with its quest to satisfy its most valuable client: Lucky Strike cigarettes.

Mad Men provided an intimate fictional examination of the historical relationship between Tobacco Road and New York's Madison Avenue advertising industry, following the flow of money from south to north and the massive influence which that money was able to buy in US popular culture through the powerful, fast-evolving medium of advertising.

The show also accomplished something unexpected for the US tobacco industry: it brought back glamorous smokers to television screens, and eventually to hundreds of millions of viewers around the globe—even if the actors weren't smoking real cigarettes. The reviews were spectacular, and awards and accolades followed. The golden age of tobacco may have been history, but the drama of the era had been resurrected to entertain American audiences.

At one of his first meetings in his new role at RJR, there was a huge bowl of cigarettes on the boardroom table—shining, unopened packs.

The lawyer stuck his hand in and started looking through the available brands, and dug past all the packs on top—Natural American Spirit. To his surprise, at the very bottom, he found one lone pack of Vantage cigarettes. The head of marketing watched him as he retrieved the pack and unwrapped the plastic.

"So you're that guy who smokes Vantage!" she said with a smile. "We don't understand this brand. It holds a 1 percent market share, with no advertising support, and at a premium price. People keep buying it, and we don't know why."

Vantage may have remained a marketing mystery, but Natural American Spirit was not. It was hard *not* to imagine how *Mad Men*'s creative genius Don Draper would have handled the account for Natural American Spirit—after all, the brand represented one possibility for where the industry was headed.

Back in 1982, three guys in New Mexico had a simple idea: create as natural a cigarette as they could, using organic tobacco and as few chemicals and additives as possible. Their company was a start-up, and the idea was smart. They weren't exactly selling hand-rolled cigarettes off a cart, but it was a humble operation compared to the major tobacco manufacturers: an independent shop that had created a unique cigarette product.

Their branding featured a bold and iconic illustration of an Indigenous American man smoking a pipe. Of course, the Indigenous branding by a company of American colonizers is exactly the kind of approach that would be disastrous in today's market. In the 1980s, though, the product was marketed to hippies and New Age smokers as an alternative to the big brands. Celebrities like Joni Mitchell and Sean Penn proudly started smoking American Spirit. The indie brand also caught the attention of the big shops.

In 2002, Reynolds bought Santa Fe Natural Tobacco, the company that made American Spirit, putting its arsenal of marketing power and experience behind this little hippy brand. Sales went vertical, as hoped. It was a good example of the industry's trend of consolidation: big fish eats smaller fish, and gets bigger.

Irony: Natural American Spirit was developed as an alternative to big tobacco products; it was the cigarette equivalent of a farmers' market, offering a more expensive and boutique product than could be found at the supers.

The marketing was complex, too.

Reynolds was trying to sell a product it wanted to suggest was better for you—because it had fewer additives—but it couldn't send that message directly, because this was a cigarette, and it was definitely bad for you. There was no such thing as a safe cigarette, so the company couldn't make any health claims about a product consumers lit on fire and inhaled.

Since the surgeon general's report, it would be an understatement to say that the American industry had been proactive in searching for and creating nicotine replacement products and alternatives. Tobacco executives all over the world had sent their R & D departments on a treasure hunt for a magical new product. Here at Reynolds, the R & D team had famously spent years and a fortune developing what they hoped would be their silver bullet —Premier—which played a starring role in the investigative book *Barbarians at the Gate* by Bryan Burrough and John Helyar, later an HBO film of the same name. It became one of the lawyer's favourite books.

Premier was a smokeless cigarette, and it lasted exactly one month on the American market, in 1988, before it was pulled off shelves. All told, it's estimated that Reynolds lost about one billion dollars on Premier. It became a valuable cautionary tale for all other tobacco companies—a tobacco ghost story, really.

Since then, it was no secret that tobacco companies were on a desperate search for safer alternatives—and so far, the customer wasn't loving any of the options. Remember what the lawyer learned R & D was trying to do on his first visit to Northern Ireland: change it up, but don't change a thing, because the customer didn't want anything to change at all.

That was the beauty, and the challenge, of Natural American Spirit: Jill and Joe Smoker were still inhaling burning tobacco but being told it didn't have as many added chemicals. In Canada it was delisted pretty fast; Health Canada rejected the marketing and branding of Natural American Spirit, although many countries did not.

American Spirit gained popularity in the US and then trended internationally. Made in the USA, shipped worldwide. And that's where the lawyer came in.

He was able to offer an international legal counsel service to an operating arm of R.J. Reynolds Global Products. Hence he became a plank in the bridge that connected Tobacco Road to the global village for this reasonably successful and newish luxury brand.

The lawyer enjoyed the work, and when he jetted to Winston-Salem, he also enjoyed getting better acquainted with US Southern culture — mostly.

Culturally, it really was different in the South.

As a Canadian of Jewish heritage, he was asked a lot of questions about his religious and political beliefs, and he learned very quickly to keep things to himself.

For example, his opinions on abortion — he was pro-choice — were met with cacophonies of laughter. His belief in universal health care: more fits of laughter. Why would the government provide medical care for free? No thank you, sir.

Thankfully, there was an overwhelming acceptance of his Jewishness. They assumed it meant he was a man of God, even if he didn't worship Jesus.

A sample conversation with a colleague went as follows.

"What church do you go to?"

"I don't. I work in Switzerland."

"Oh, well, which church do you go to in Switzerland?"

"I don't."

"Well, why not?"

"Because I'm Jewish."

"Oh, well, which synagogue?"

Everyone seemed to know the terminology and framework for Judaism. They knew what the High Holidays were. To have a faith seemed to be important here. It provided context as to who the lawyer was as a professional—what his core values were. His peers were more concerned about someone being a man of God rather than being specifically Christian. Indeed, many of his colleagues would say grace or pray before a meal, and he would kind of go along with it and look down at the table.

Amen. He passed the religious values test.

Sadly, when it came to sports, there was no talking soccer. These guys were into NASCAR and basketball. There was no professional sports team in the Greensboro area, but there were tickets to see the local university team, Wake Forest, play basketball.

This wasn't an old English tobacco company, and it wasn't the Japanese government pretending to be a tobacco company. This was R.J. Reynolds: reclining outside in the melting sun, sipping a mint julep, making room for the barbecue that was on the way.

His hotel was called the Winston-Salem Marriott. There was even an elevator operator there—and, yes, he was African American, and the lawyer believed his name was actually Winston. Winston was incredibly warm to the lawyer, every day. The lawyer observed that all of the faces in the executive office were white, while many of the service staff in town, and the workers on the lines in the Tobaccoville factory, were African American.

It seemed to him that the South still hadn't received the memo that segregation was over. This suspicion spilled over into conversations with fellow colleagues, who, with very few exceptions, were devout, God-fearing Republican Christians, and who seemed happy to drink the Old South Kool-Aid—or mint julep, if you will.

George W. Bush was still president, but he was approaching the end of his second term. On the horizon, there was a young senator from Chicago who was coming on strong. Barack Obama was out there touring the country with his "Fire It Up" speech—which was funny, if you were a smoker. Obama, in fact, was a smoker, but everyone down here knew that his love of cigarettes wouldn't stop him from coming down hard on the industry if he was voted into the Oval Office. Obama was just another storm cloud on the horizon for Big Tobacco.

It was easy to forget that Washington, DC, was really a Southern town.

Smoking had been permitted—perhaps even encouraged—at the White House all the way up until Hillary Clinton became first lady. She was the one who banned smoking in the White House —yes, even cigars.

Out at dinner one evening, the lawyer was chatting with a board member of a major Southern-based tobacco company and politely asked him who he was going to vote for in the upcoming presidential election. Clearly, it was a mistake to ask.

The man was powerful and Ivy League educated—including the mandatory MBA—and he was on the board of a Fortune 250 company. The man put down his knife and fork, looked at the lawyer in a horrified way, and said this.

"There is no way I'm voting to put a _____ in the White House."

The lawyer tried to keep his cool, but it was shocking. This person was senior to him in the industry and an influential leader in the business community. The lawyer suddenly felt naive; he hadn't actually believed this kind of ignorance still existed or that such a racial slur would be uttered openly, completely unfiltered. It was a wake-up call. It could be ugly just beneath the surface here.

That's why it was so refreshing to meet the Legend. He was the counterbalance the lawyer needed in his new cultural environment.

The Legend was unlike any other lawyer he met working for his new tobacco company—or for any tobacco company.

The lawyer had first encountered him in 2001, on a long-distance business trip to Winston-Salem, when he was a junior lawyer at the British company.

At that time, his company was negotiating a joint venture with R.J. Reynolds in Switzerland. Mary was the lead lawyer on the deal, and he happened to be the lawyer tasked with managing the relationship once the papers were signed. The Legend stuck out, in his style and his substance.

Most legal departments in the US had a uniform: well-pressed chinos and expensive collared shirts, jacket, and sometimes tie, depending. The Legend wore a tie-dye T-shirt, had several piercings in one ear, kind of messy hair, and his long face was often punctuated with a great big cigar hanging off his lip. His colleagues often compared his long, imposing face to Joe Camel's. The Legend was a New York Jew. He was pro–civil rights and also took the concept of freedom of expression quite seriously.

The lawyer immediately felt a bond with him.

Over that week in 2001, he started to get to know the Legend. Those types of negotiations were never just about signing one piece of paper; it was a lot of work, and they spent real time together.

The first time the lawyer visited the Legend's office, he noted a stack of pornographic magazines on his desk, right out in the open. Even though he was in his early sixties at that point, he had a youthful energy and a booming voice. Talking to the Legend was like having a conversation with a radio announcer.

"I bet you're wondering what those are there for," the Legend said, raising his eyebrow, when he saw the lawyer had noticed the magazines. "I have the greatest job in the world: this company pays me to read pornography at work. Why? you may ask. It's one of the last types of magazines we're allowed to legally advertise in, after the Master Settlement Agreement. Because we're guaranteed an adult audience: you have to be eighteen years of age to buy these."

Also present in the Legend's office: a small putting green; a life-sized version of the gopher from the movie *Caddyshack*; and stacks and stacks of paper. The Legend was what some would refer to as old school. His computer wasn't even on his desk.

Not surprisingly, the Legend unsettled his colleagues: he was nothing like the Southern gentleman professional stereotype, because, indeed, he was from a different tradition—the brash, loud, New York Jewish lawyer. And, yes, he was a member of the small Jewish community down South (so there *was* a Jewish community here), where he attended synagogue. In fact, he donated significant financial support to a Holocaust research and archival project at a nearby university.

The Legend liked Chinese food—shocker—so they often indulged together. They had a lot in common. The Legend had three boys who were around the lawyer's age, and he suspected this reinforced their relationship.

In the years that followed, they had become quite close, travelling together on various business trips for conferences and then starting to hang out as friends. The Legend introduced the younger lawyer to a number of colleagues in the industry, and if he was ever in Europe over the High Holidays, they'd attend services at synagogues in Lausanne or Geneva.

The young lawyer considered him a mentor, and it turned out the Legend was watching his back. While the lawyer had been twiddling his thumbs at his desk in Switzerland after the Japanese takeover, wondering when he'd have to walk the plank with his colleagues, it was the Legend who had suggested to Reynolds that they snap him up.

The Legend knew the industry through and through, and was always prepared to defend it and its Southern roots. He'd started working at Reynolds in the late 1970s, so he was there throughout the Premier era; he was there for the sale of the international business to Japan Tobacco; and he'd played a role in the Master Settlement Agreement, with a seat at the table in New York, face to face with the states' attorneys general.

It was rumoured that at one of those meetings, he'd pulled out a Joe Camel mask during the negotiations and put it on. For pulling that eccentric stunt, he'd come close to being fired. Just one reason why he was "the Legend."

"We're all going to jail," boomed the Legend.

It was a saying he loved to use at the end of a meeting, while shaking hands after signing a deal. His other closer, even more inside baseball, was "See you in Bermuda." Bermuda was where lawyers often went for arbitration between parties if a deal turned sour. It took confidence to deliver that line after signing a contract.

"We're all going to jail" was self-explanatory: a nod to a *Twilight Zone* future when law enforcement showed up to cart tobacco executives off to some international court to stand trial for the sins of their industry. The seemingly sardonic tagline was part of the psychological defence system the Legend had constructed in response to the surreal arc of changing social attitude he'd witnessed over his professional career in tobacco.

Keep in mind that the Legend had started in the industry before the younger lawyer was even born. He had lived through all of those cataclysmic events stemming from the surgeon general's waves, so, from his perspective, "We're all going to jail" could conceivably have been the next logical chapter for tobacco employees. Certainly, this fear of growing social persecution would have kept him awake some nights. The world had completely transformed around him.

The lawyer, meanwhile, had joined the industry years after it had already been vilified. He sometimes thought back to those interview questions in his session with the headhunter Heather and Mary. Heather had asked him about whether he was comfortable doing anything illegal: his firm answer was that he was *not* comfortable doing anything illegal. This was the response Mary had wanted to hear, because it was the image the industry so urgently wanted to cultivate: law-abiding, responsible.

So far, by the way, there had not been a single case of a tobacco executive ever going to prison, since any legal battles related to smoking were tried in civil court, not as criminal cases

The Legend, really, was a pirate at heart—an iconoclast who was infused with that 1960s American spirit of being deeply committed to the idea of questioning authority and challenging the status quo. Often, when they had travelled together, the Legend would repeat to the younger lawyer, "Question everything and trust no one."

It was one way for the old pirate to pass his rebel spirit on to his protégé. Sadly, the Legend officially retired on the day the lawyer started at the new company.

The lawyer arrived back in the US just in time to watch the American economy crumble. He was in the Winston-Salem office the day that Lehman Brothers went bankrupt—on September 15, 2008—and the stock market just kept diving deeper.

It was terrible news for the US, and for the world.

Oddly, no one at the company seemed very worried about the recession.

The tobacco industry, it turned out, was unusually resilient during recessionary times. There were a few reasons for this, he learned. Smokers tended to smoke more when times were tough; stress and anxiety made hands reach for cigarettes.

Meanwhile, the company was profitable and fiscally responsible.

It had filled its silos with cash in case of a rainy day; it was always forecasting rain in a world where it was under attack. Best of all, Wall Street, even as its towers were littered with pink slips, viewed tobacco stocks as solid, defensive investments—safe vaults to protect wealth during uncertain times.

After all, this industry had survived multiple attacks and continued to thrive in a hostile environment. The stock market crash might have little adverse effect on a cash-rich business that catered to customers addicted to its products, and which fed their pleasure receptors during painful times.

The lawyer heard some chatter among upper management about the dropping values of their personal investments and 401(k)s, but no one was worried about the effects of the recession on the company or the industry.

This was surprising to the lawyer, considering the potential long-term effects of the Master Settlement Agreement (MSA) on the entire US industry—the agreement the Legend had helped negotiate. No one actually knew what implications the settlement would ultimately have.

On the surface, readers who scanned news headlines about the ongoing assault on the tobacco industry would have received the intended message: the government was prevailing, and it continued to deal blows to tobacco company profits, with smoking rates in steady decline. Smoking was being banned in more and more public spaces, packs were becoming more expensive, and tobacco's marketing and advertising capabilities were drastically diminished. Plus, the industry continued to be punished with the MSA—an Old Testament punishment, really—that $200 billion being paid to Uncle Sam over a period of twenty-five years: financial pain inflicted over decades.

The MSA was the mortgage from hell—one without an end date. That $200 billion dollars was just an estimate of the bill owing by Big

Tobacco for the *first* twenty-five years after the agreement was signed. In fact, payments were directed to continue "in perpetuity," meaning that as long as cigarettes were sold in the US by those companies, money would be owed annually to government. The agreement lasted as long as there were fire-breathers in America: essentially, forever, or until every cigarette company that had signed on to the MSA was no longer manufacturing sticks.

It would have been a doomsday scenario for most products, right?

The Legend and the other formidable tobacco lawyers who were around that table with the attorneys general were not stupid. They had ascended to their highly paid senior legal positions for a reason: they were experienced, shrewd, and they were representing Fortune 250 and Fortune 500 companies with immense influence.

The challenge with this kind of negotiation in the US was that it had to be constitutional. That's why everyone was sitting down at a table together to work it out politely.

The United States Constitution was crystal clear about freedom of speech. The law couldn't apply an unconstitutional request to a consumer product which was legal and still beloved by millions. That's why it was called an agreement and not a law, because an agreement can't be unconstitutional if it's agreed to by everyone involved.

The top lawyers for major US tobacco companies got down to work and chipped away at the attorneys general, and the agreement they shaped was an outcome their companies, and in some cases their shareholders, could genuinely find pleasing. It was signed by all parties in November 1998. Hands were shaken — the lawyer could picture the Legend muttering, "We're all going to jail" — and the price was set. It was called the Master Settlement Agreement because it was the agreement to end all other agreements, past and future.

Consider the following: smoking rates in the US had hit their peak in the mid-1950s, when about 45 percent of the American adult population smoked. By the 1970s, those numbers had dropped just slightly, to about 40 percent. By 1990, though, the rate had hit 30 percent, and it continued to go down. By 2008, the smoking rate was closer to 20 percent—which meant there were still forty-six million American smokers.

Various US states were continuing the process of banning smoking from public spaces, and, as planned, the price of a pack was steadily rising across the country. New York State had raised its tobacco price to about ten dollars a pack at that time, and this was the new reality: pay more for a legal consumer product.

On the surface, the industry was being punished for its sins, but it wasn't really so bad. Sure, the stock prices of publicly listed Big Tobacco companies decreased, but only slightly.

And when prices started to rise on a pack of cigarettes, it wasn't because of a tax: it was a hike that funded the MSA payments. That's how the agreement got around taxing the product in a way that was palatable to corporate American values. But there was a hidden opportunity with MSA price increases: the margin a manufacturer could charge became greater too.

Remember, once upon a time, a pack of sticks was about twenty-five cents to make at the factory: dried leaves and paper. Even in the good old days, when a pack was selling for a dollar, tobacco companies were making an excellent profit margin. When the price went up because of the MSA, tobacco companies raised their prices as well, by only a few pennies at a time. You may think a penny or two is nothing, but multiply it by tens of millions of packs and it adds up.

The best part was the blame factor: Jill and Joe Smoker always thought, "Wow, the government is ripping me off." But in reality, it was a team effort; the government and the tobacco companies were both raising the price on each pack sold.

This unlikely alliance resulted in the following counterintuitive outcome: tobacco companies were selling fewer packs of sticks but making more money per pack. They were still winning. The governments were generating income by receiving their MSA payments. They were winning too. The product was still available on your corner, and it was still 100 percent legal to American consumers.

Meanwhile, there was another benefit to the industry.

All government litigation stopped. From that angle alone, tobacco companies were now saving tens of millions of dollars on lawyers' fees, and they were no longer under threat of complete obliteration from the courts.

Advertising was almost impossible, but it was exactly the same challenge for all competitors, so it was a level playing field when it came to ad restrictions.

The players hit hardest by those restrictions were actually the ad agencies, along with magazines, cultural and sporting organizations, and television networks. No more cash from Big Tobacco.

And after having paid a fortune to Madison Avenue for decades, and helping to pioneer huge changes in the medium of advertising itself, Big Tobacco in America was now released from its addiction to ads. The industry began saving hundreds of millions of dollars a year.

In a way, the MSA was the perfect dramatic epilogue to the *Mad Men* saga playing out on American television sets. Basically, all of those supersized accounts with Big Tobacco, which had helped feed the growth of the ad industry, simply ended.

For decades in West Hollywood, at the corner of Sunset Boulevard and Marmont Lane—which curls up to the posh enclave of the Chateau Marmont hotel—a seventy-foot billboard of the Marlboro Man had loomed over the epicentre of "cool." For the millions of

La-La Landers perpetually speeding to the next power lunch, this spectral cowboy rising on Sunset was almost as overpowering and ever-present as sunlight.

Then in 1999, in line with the MSA, a crew of workers showed up to dismantle the Marlboro Man. The cowboy was replaced by a more updated image, which better represented the brighter, innovative future ahead: Apple.

That same year, TNT released *Pirates of Silicon Valley*, the first movie made about the battle for tech innovation in America—these computer nerds seemed to be the new corporate pirates, conquering from digital oceans. And on cue Hollywood took one of its only big swipes against the tobacco industry with the release of *The Insider*. And even though Russell Crowe was playing Jeffery Wigand on screen, the actor was smoking two packs a day while he shot the film. He later confided to *Time* magazine about his addiction, "I'm smart enough to acknowledge it but too stupid to stop."

In the unfolding story of Big Tobacco and Hollywood, only two major studio movies—*The Insider* and *Thank You for Smoking*—were ever produced in which Big Tobacco was publicly flogged.

When television networks had stopped selling ads to tobacco companies back in the 1970s, their strategy had pivoted to product placement—mostly in Hollywood films. But the MSA language was clear on this point: no more paying to showcase cigarette brands in movies. That was over now.

Meanwhile, the very act of smoking in movies became entwined with the rating system. If your movie had smoking in it—or nudity or swearing—it automatically received an Adult rating, or R rating, just one reason fake IDs for teenagers continued to be essential at the box office.

What was truly shocking, though, was that after the MSA, cigarettes managed a grand return to smaller screens in American living rooms. "If you don't like what's being said, change the conversation," said *Mad Men's* Don Draper, and that's exactly what happened when it came to smoking on American television.

Despite more than a decade of US broadcasters agreeing to curtail incidents of smoking in television shows, sticks had made an unlikely comeback—and it went far beyond "the smoking man" in *The X-Files* or rebellious teenagers in *Twin Peaks*, both of which shows aired after 9 P.M., the "watershed line," meaning that programs with mature content could only air after that hour.

This smoking revival may have been surprising to some viewers—especially parents and anti-smoking advocates—but here's why it made sense: in the same way that Big Tobacco had been freed from its bonds to advertisers, so had HBO.

Home Box Office was a newish "premium" subscriber-based TV service born in the 1970s but which came of age in the 1990s. Its business model meant it wasn't subject to the same pressures to "be nice" as its US network predecessors were under, because it didn't feature ads in between its movies. It wasn't trying to please advertising partners by censoring content.

In fact, when HBO created an episodic drama division, it promised edgier storytelling—more like R-rated movies, for sophisticated adults—and part of that edge included showing a world where people smoked.

HBO's first dramatic series, which launched in 1997, was called *Oz*. It was a gritty one-hour prison drama where sticks were used as currency as well as a way to kill time pleasurably while serving it.

Then in 1999, one year into the MSA, HBO introduced the world to Tony Soprano, who chomped on his big cigar as he fought for control of his profitable Italian American business empire, which, similarly to Big Tobacco, was under constant threat of government assault, with its glory days long gone.

About his panic attacks, Tony explained to his new shrink, "It's good to be in something on the ground floor. . . . I came too late for that, I know. . . . But lately I'm getting the feeling that I came in at the end. The best is over."

"Many Americans, I think, feel that way," his psychiatrist responded sympathetically.

Of course, Tony could easily have been talking about the contemporary tobacco industry.

The Sopranos was widely considered the most critically acclaimed television show of its era. It was groundbreaking, and its anti-hero seduced US audiences into paying for this new model of subscriber-based television. Exhaling smoke, Tony dispensed this piece of hard-earned gangster wisdom about the true nature of Western capitalism: "Sometimes you have to give people the illusion of control."

In 2007 as *The Sopranos* wrapped its final season and *Mad Men* arrived in its stylish cloud of smoke, a quirky, struggling company called Netflix—which had been delivering DVDs for rent through the mail system—started streaming content directly to audiences via the internet.

Netflix was a subscriber-based model as well, and like HBO, it was mostly hocking movies with zero ads. Within a decade of streaming, though, it was soon promising more of what HBO and AMC had been delivering: edgy, episodic content that wasn't at the mercy of old network values or advertising pressure to tone it down. In fact, Netflix wasn't even pretending to be a television station: it was a "platform," and its home was the World Wide Web.

The internet wasn't even mentioned in the MSA, and there were no rules concerning tobacco displays, advertising, or imagery when it came to the expanding constellations of the dot-com universe. This was good news for tobacco.

When the lawyer started jetting regularly to Winston-Salem, the industry was ten years into the MSA agreement. By then, the market capitalization of Reynolds American was holding strong at about

$40 billion, and that figure was for the number two tobacco company in the US; Philip Morris had even deeper pockets.

In fact, all three major US tobacco companies were managing to navigate the tumultuous waves of the Surgeon General's Warning and the MSA—smoothly, drawing minimal attention—thanks to the attorneys general, lawyers like the Legend, and the spirit of American capitalism.

Here's a question: What's more effective: a commercial for cigarettes which appeared alongside a show, or Don Draper at the *centre* of a show looking icy cool while he smoked a Lucky Strike after sex or closing the latest big deal? Rumour had it that sales of Lucky Strike had increased by 50 percent during *Mad Men*'s run.

Even after the MSA had stipulated there would be no advertising of cigarettes in televised ads or product placement in films, and while the tobacco companies were technically holding up their end of this agreement, smoke poured back into the vastly influential medium, and the popular new TV programming platforms were now being consumed globally. By 2010, the smoking rate in the US was holding steady at just under 20 percent, or more than forty million fire-breathers.

In the opening episodes of America's twenty-first century, the anti-smoking lobby, the government, and the tobacco companies were all winning: the tobacco paradox surged across the land of the free.

Even as his company prospered at home and abroad, the lawyer knew his own international tobacco story arc was coming to an end.

As a general rule, the ultimate purpose of any high-level expat employee was to move into a foreign market, set up the shop to run efficiently, and eventually make themselves redundant by finding a qualified local to do the job. Expats were expensive, after all.

Case in point: while in Switzerland, the lawyer often had to stay in a hotel in Zurich two or three nights a week, all at the expense of the company.

He felt less like a pirate and more like an astronaut, floating out there all alone in his satellite office in Switzerland, wondering how much longer he'd be kept on in this capacity.

Sure enough, after about a year and a half, Reynolds decided to put a local into his job. He was being phased out. *Auf wiedersehen*, *au revoir*, and *ciao*, Switzerland.

Where to sail to next?

The company asked him and his family to relocate permanently to Winston-Salem. He talked it over with his wife, and neither of them were keen on making that move. The culture was too much of a leap for them, and it didn't feel right.

He searched for another option, re-examining the fine print of his contract. He found there was a clause that required the company to pay for him to move wherever he wanted to go if he left his job. He and his wife talked it through, and they decided it was time to sail north.

So, instead of jetting to Winston-Salem, he stepped down from his role. There were no hard feelings.

He was almost as high up the legal corporate chain as you could climb, save for being general counsel. And even from this altitude at the company, the exit experience was just like the entrance: icy and smooth, zero friction. He remembered the ice water Heather the headhunter sipped quietly throughout his first interview with her all those years ago in London.

It was like that: clinical and cold. Sign here, a firm handshake, a polite smile. Nice to meet you, thank you for your service—goodbye.

DON'T HOLD YOUR BREATH

Have you ever visited Toronto? The world is here.

The lawyer was thirty-six years old and unemployed when he flashed his Canadian passport to a Toronto border agent at Pearson International Airport, flanked by his wife and two children.

"Welcome home," the agent said.

He'd been gone for eighteen years: first for university, then the journalism foray, followed by law school, the boutique law firm, and the tobacco odyssey. He had exited this city solo and now, in 2010, was returning as part of a family unit, as well as quietly importing his experiences of working in one of the most contentious industries in history.

He'd been a corporate pirate and sailed the seven seas. Now, the lawyer was lowering the skull and crossbones and raising the red maple leaf.

Thankfully, during those years of absence, his hometown on the southern edge of Canada had transformed and was surging with vibrant communities and cultural DNA from almost every country around the globe, which meant that whatever food he loved could easily be acquired here in "The Six" as Drake—one of the city's most well-known export brands—had famously called it.

Iranian food, yes. Mongolian café, yes. Ethiopian, check. Vietnamese, practically on every corner. Sushi, the same. Nigerian, Peruvian, Russian? Yep. Italian, fuhgedaboutit—from which region in Italy were you craving culinary delights? Chinese, c'mon. Fifty bucks could buy you a feast at his favourite dim sum spot in Chinatown.

The Six hadn't always been like this.

Toronto was a famously conservative town for much of its history, but over his lifetime it seemed to have added some new muscle—with sinews of power and influence binding it to the global village.

In a lot of ways Toronto had the opposite vibe of Winston-Salem: it was an international metropolis with a thriving downtown core, and still growing fast. He immediately noticed the flock of construction cranes perched over the cityscape and hundreds of glossy new condo developments—along with a few neighbourhoods he didn't even recognize. The sprawl was punctuated by the futuristic-looking CN Tower, which somehow made it all feel like a city with a bright future ahead.

Of course, there were still smokers here too, but they were harder to spot and seemed more akin to pieces of the city's vanishing heritage buildings: old brick walls slated for demolition.

This was because Canada—often so humble about its achievements—had quietly evolved to be a leader in the world's anti-smoking crusade.

He and his wife felt the attitude change immediately, as they settled into their new life in a leafy, upscale Toronto neighbourhood and subscribed to *Toronto Life* and *Macleans* magazines. He also traded in his trustee old Nokia cell for a new product trending in personal communication: an iPhone meant he could now scan headlines from the *Globe and Mail*, *National Post*, *Toronto Star*, and CBC News while lining up at the grocery store: so convenient.

There was, though, one factor in their new life that was less than convenient: in the UK, in Switzerland, and in the Southern US, no one had particularly cared that he worked for a tobacco company. Here, though, it was crystal clear the couple were being judged by their new peers.

When the girls enrolled in school, a parent told him off at a school social function after asking what he did for a living.

Even some members of his own family took umbrage. At a bar mitzvah, he was cornered by an older relative who also happened to be a quite successful and well-respected corporate lawyer. It was an abrasive and condescending conversation. While others caught up on family news, this older man expounded on the evils of the tobacco industry: that it was immoral to work for such an atrocious industry; that, basically, such a career was an abject failure and an outrage to the profession of law.

"You should be ashamed of yourself," the relative stated bluntly.

He could almost hear the Legend booming, "We're all going to jail."

The lawyer absorbed the family abuse and then snuck outside for a cigarette, but even that was tougher to do in Canada. Smoking had long been banned in public indoor spaces, then on patios, and now he was having to hide in alleyways to inhale in peace, away from the cold eyes of judgmental citizens and the officious red circles of No Smoking signs.

It really caught the couple off guard, this social righteousness.

At first, the lawyer simply tried to ignore it, but he was also fascinated by its genesis. The social climate was so different from when he'd grown up here.

What accounted for the seismic attitude change?

———

In Toronto—as across much of Canada—the lawyer noted that when it came to tobacco tastes, the deep roots in colonial British culture had somehow managed to survive the powerful influence of the US market: the giant next door.

Canadians flocked to Hollywood movies, danced to American music, watched American TV shows, subscribed to American newspapers and magazines, but, oddly, they still smoked British cigarettes: Rothmans, Player's, and Du Maurier were the reigning brands here and were purchased with currency still brandishing the image of the Queen.

And no offence, but his Canadian compatriots didn't seem to know very much about the origins of their chosen brands.

The lawyer enjoyed casual encounters with Canuck smokers, especially men who smoked Du Maurier. If given the opportunity, he'd explain that Du Maurier originated in Britain as a women's brand of cigarette and that it had been delisted in the UK for twenty-five years; many Canadian fire-breathers believed it was an iconic, created-in-Canada brand.

Zoom out from one brand to look at the landscape of companies, and the picture was similar. In Canada, there were no truly Canadian tobacco companies left.

Consolidation was the rule here too—along with ring-fencing.

There were three major tobacco companies in Canada, now all owned by larger multinational corporations: Imperial Tobacco, maker of Du Maurier and Player's, was owned by British American Tobacco, headquartered in the UK; Macdonald, maker of Export A, was owned by Japan Tobacco International, headquartered in Switzerland, as you know; and Rothmans, Benson & Hedges was owned by Philip Morris International, also headquartered in Switzerland, as you know.

Here at home, Imperial, Macdonald, and Rothmans, Benson & Hedges—the Three Smokes, let's call them—once wielded massive influence across this vast, resource-rich country, but the golden age of tobacco was long gone in Canada, and the influence of these companies was clearly in decline, as was their customer base. He'd spy other lonely smokers loitering in the shadows of office buildings, like astronauts floating outside a space station; it took one to know one.

When the lawyer strolled to his corner store to buy a pack, he was shocked to see the cigarettes were now hidden out of sight inside metal storage cabinets. He was really taken aback.

A new law had recently come into effect in the province of Ontario that prohibited the display of cigarettes in convenience stores. Because tobacco advertising had been illegal in Canada for some time, those packs behind the counter at eye level were really the last place a consumer was confronted by the once ubiquitous brands.

Now that precious last window had closed, a smoker had to know which brand to ask for, or that they were even available for purchase. He thought about Ben on the drive team, rearranging those convenience kingdom shelves all those years ago. Eye-level influence: gone.

The lawyer had travelled to dozens of countries on behalf of the tobacco industry and studied each nation's shifting tobacco laws and regulations, but he'd never seen an environment as cold and inhospitable towards smokers as this one.

So, what did it take for a country to change the social behaviour of its population?

Canada proved it required decades of focus, hundreds of millions of dollars, a multi-pronged strategy, and resolve: playing the long game.

Only through this national, coordinated, and sustained assault was it possible for the government to deeply alter social attitudes in a relatively short time—about one generation. His generation, in fact.

But the genesis of the Canadian anti-smoking strategy had occurred before he was born.

It had begun during the 1960s, in the golden age when more than half of Canadian adults smoked. In the summer of 1963 — before the US surgeon general weighed in — Canada's federal minister of health, Judy LaMarsh, did something very brave. She stood up in the House of Commons and announced that there was evidence linking smoking to lung cancer. Her statement caused a small wave, which gathered strength less than a year later when the surgeon general dropped the bad-news bomb on America.

Connected to this developing news story on tobacco was the fact that in the 1960s, Canada chose to divert from the reigning US-based model of delivering medical care to the population via private health insurers. Instead, the country embarked on a massive transition, eventually centralizing how its citizens paid for medicine. By the 1970s, all of the country's provinces and territories had adopted some form of public health care — which was why the lawyer had possessed a Canadian health care card since birth.

Then in 1984, the Canada Health Act was passed, enshrining into law what was already a reality for most Canadians: paying taxes to fund the majority of their medical services (unfortunately, excluding dental, much to the regret and consternation of the Canadian populace).

Of course, this "universal" health care system was at odds with the damage smoking was inflicting on the well-being of so many citizens (and that's aside from the out-of-pocket cost to Canadians of cleaning nicotine stains off their teeth). Government surveys were sent out, information on tobacco use was collected and analyzed, and strategies were formed.

By the time the lawyer was attending that memorable anti-smoking seminar in his elementary school gymnasium, circa 1985, one-third of adults were still smoking.

Over the next twenty-five years, Canada exerted more energy and more funding to empower its citizens to butt out. It began with some preliminary legislation: no more lighting up in federal offices or on the national airline. These laws began the process of controlling the movement of smokers, adjusting their behaviour, and ever so slightly shifting the public's attitude to fire-breathing.

During the lawyer's years abroad, tobacco companies in Canada were ordered to list on their packs the yield levels of tar and carbon monoxide, methodically measured by the many-mouthed machines in R & D labs across the world. Then legislation took aim at ensuring a bright, healthy future for the country's youth: no selling cigarettes to anyone under eighteen, and please unplug those cigarette vending machines, because they were no longer legal; kids couldn't just put change into a machine and receive sticks.

Attacking the brands came next, when big black-and-white health warnings on packs became mandatory: "SMOKING CAN KILL YOU"; "CIGARETTES ARE ADDICTIVE"; "TOBACCO SMOKE CAN HARM YOUR CHILDREN." The lawyer recalled returning to university in London from family holidays home and gawking with his UK friends at the absurdly large Canadian warnings.

Canada's government kept probing the industry to see how far it could push before the Three Smokes pushed back. It made its biggest play in 1997 with the Tobacco Act, which at the time was the most aggressive anti-smoking legislation ever introduced in the world, banning all advertising and all sponsorship. Well ahead of the US anti-smoking curve.

The lawyer remembered how, roving around Toronto as a teen, he saw the way branding was baked into the logos at the Du Maurier Jazz Festival, the Benson & Hedges Symphony of Fire (fireworks displays), and the awards shows promoted by the Matinée Fashion Foundation. Millions of sponsorship dollars fed these popular gatherings and festivals.

The Three Smokes finally decided to swing back, together.

They did so by taking the government to court over the proposed act, and any semblance of goodwill that may have been left between the feds and the tobacco industry went up in smoke. That legal challenge wound its way to Canada's Supreme Court—and the Three Smokes lost the case. The Supremes sided with the government.

As the new millennium opened, Canada launched its "Tobacco Strategy" and soon became the first country in the world to legislate pictorial health warnings onto cigarette packages.

These often gruesome, memorable images occupied 50 percent of every pack: "SMOKING CAUSES IMPOTENCE," one warning simply stated, accompanied by a large photo of a cigarette drooping downward in sexual defeat—clever, effective, and it stuck in your mind.

The large, pictorial warnings were revolutionary—and at that point in consumer history, no one, anywhere in global capital markets, had ever witnessed this kind of treatment of a popular consumer product that was 100 percent legal.

Canada was leading the way, and forty-two other countries went on to mandate pictorial health warnings on cigarette packages.

And Canada always seemed to go further, first: it not only banned cigarette advertising on television, it created its own anti-smoking ads and broadcast them in prime-time slots once so prized by tobacco companies. One of those commercials was narrated by Heather Crowe, a waitress who had worked for decades in a restaurant where the air was blue with smoke. Crowe had been diagnosed with lung cancer, but she had never smoked a single cigarette in her life. Now she was dying, she bluntly told Canadians.

It was a personal and powerful story.

And there was support available: any smoker who panicked after watching Crowe tell her story could call a quit-smoking helpline.

In some Canadian provinces, doctors began giving patients access to free nicotine replacement drugs, as did the Centre for Addiction and Mental Health, a global leader in addiction research, at its nicotine clinic in Toronto.

The Canadian government kept on pushing the product back, and winning.

By the time the lawyer's family was acclimatizing to their new northern home, Canada's smoking rate had dipped to historic lows not seen since the pre-war era: under 20 percent, and trending downward.

Most Canadians likely believed it was a terrible time to be in the tobacco business in Canada, although the tobacco paradox was unfolding here too.

One mechanism being used by the government to dissuade smokers was far more contentious than any other law or restriction: taxes.

In 1985, a pack of cigarettes cost roughly one dollar. From that point on—with only a few exceptions—the Canadian government raised the taxes on cigarettes once a year, and sometimes more often. By 2010, the price of a pack, including tax, had climbed to over ten dollars, and it would continue to rise. Cigarettes were becoming a luxury item, and, of course, those taxes were feeding provincial and federal coffers with billions of dollars annually. A fortune.

The price hike did work, though. It targeted Jill and Joe Smoker's disposable income, and therefore their ability to afford cigarettes. The World Health Organization agreed with the strategy, suggesting it should be adopted by every nation.

The challenge, as the lawyer perceived it, was that even when you raised taxes, very few smokers dropped out along the way. It's true that fewer people would smoke, but most fire-breathers would simply pay whatever what was being demanded to get their fix.

And there was blowback too, remember. Raising taxes on cigarettes fuelled that black market for sticks. Think of the man with gleaming shoes in Spain and his cross-border clientele.

Addiction was a powerful motivator, and smokers always found a way.

Rising taxes also became a hidden opportunity for the Three Smokes—just as it had for the US industry—to add a few cents to their base pack price whenever those government tax increases occurred. Even with smoking rates in steep decline, this allowed the Three Smokes to earn more profit on every pack sold than ever before. Even better: the government got the blame. So everyone was winning in this northern arena too.

Except for the consumer. They were always losing.

It seemed as if the tobacco paradox would continue to play out smoothly in Canada: the price of a pack would keep rising; the percentage of smokers would slowly decrease; No Smoking signs would continue to proliferate; and the government would receive its massive tobacco paycheck.

Then two separate events occurred that were truly shocking to the lawyer.

First, the change in Canadian social attitudes towards tobacco had an effect on him.

And then Canadians started winning court cases against tobacco companies.

You never actually quit smoking. You're just no longer smoking. But it's not true that people can't give it up—millions do.

After a bit of time back in Canada, the lawyer decided to smoke his last cigarette. He chose to do it in the same place where he'd smoked his first: on his parents' back porch, within view of the garage where he'd lit up so many years ago.

He'd started before high school. Then he'd upped his consumption in university and transformed into a chain-smoker, a champion smoker. And unlike most people who smoked, he'd been given access to a free supply for ten years and worked in an environment that was incredibly supportive of his habit. How many people actually got to smoke professionally for a living?

There were so many ways to quit: the patch, gum, drugs, lasers, hypnosis, therapy, e-cigarettes. When the lawyer decided to stop, he chose cold turkey. He was just that kind of guy. He didn't even use Allen Carr's *Easy Way to Stop Smoking*—but power to you if you do. He's heard it works.

Instead, he thought about gambling, and he thought about his odds.

Nobody really knew what was going to happen after they'd smoked all those cigarettes, because smoking was a gamble.

It was a game smokers played.

You were dealing with questions of probability—about the way your body was able to withstand the effects of tobacco smoke. It wasn't equal odds for everyone, though. It just didn't work like that. The truth was you might never have to pay the piper. And if you did, it might not be until many years later, after you'd quit. The harmful effects of smoking were not always felt immediately; the pain could come much later, and for some never at all. That's why it was a gamble.

It was scary to think about it, but he liked his odds.

He was out of the industry and he had come full circle, right back to his very start, standing on his parent's back porch, smoking cigarettes. This time, he wasn't hiding from his parents. For Christ's sake, he'd worked for the tobacco industry!

Now, he was hiding from his children.

He never smoked in front of the kids, and that was one of the reasons for giving it up. As far as he was aware, they had never seen him smoke a cigarette, but he didn't want to have a conversation with them in the future that he knew he would lose.

"Daddy, why are you doing something that's going to kill you?"

None of his legal training and none of the corporate affairs bullshit he'd picked up over the years had prepared him for this; he just couldn't use those skills on his kids.

Children were taught at school that tobacco companies were monsters. And that smoking would kill you. Anti-smoking education, especially for young children, had become very harsh and very definite in the message it delivered.

In Canada, the twenty-year evolution in smoking regulations had been seismic. There was nowhere to hide, not even on his parents' back porch. He felt like he couldn't smoke anywhere, and when he did, it felt wrong. It was like sitting on public transport reading a copy of *Penthouse*; people looked at you in a very peculiar and often judgmental way.

His friends and social circle had similar attitudes: "How could you work for that industry?"

The whole self-righteous attitude bugged him and his wife, because he wasn't doing anything wrong, and he wasn't doing anything illegal, but just by transplanting their family from Switzerland to Canada, his smoking and his career seemed to be big problems for everyone. So he decided to give up smoking.

He'd believed, from the very first day he started working in the industry, that the addictiveness of tobacco products was not insurmountable. When he made his decision to give up smoking permanently, with pressure from his wife and mother, he stopped. Just like that.

He smoked his last cigarette. He breathed in, and exhaled. He stubbed it out, and he told himself he was done.

And despite what Allen Carr had to say, it wasn't easy.

The problem was the withdrawal symptoms were excruciating.

First and foremost, he started eating, more and more. If there ever was a benefit of smoking, its effect as an appetite suppressant had got to be it. It wasn't coincidental that runway models smoked like chimneys, and he started to put on weight.

Sleep was another challenge.

For about six months he stared at the ceiling from midnight until 3 A.M. every night. The gnawing pain of withdrawal wouldn't let him sleep. It felt like a hangover that never went away. From midnight to 3 A.M. was when all of your worst fears arrived, invading your imagination and dancing in the darkness of the mind. No wonder they called it the witching hour.

To this day, he has not slept through the night, and he has resigned himself to the fact that he may never sleep through the night again.

But the health benefits were immediate.

His breathing improved dramatically.

His sense of smell and taste improved dramatically. He was, for example, able to smell tobacco on other people in a much more heightened way.

He noticed that his heart rate decreased.

He didn't sweat nearly as much. He hardly perspired at all during the day.

What he missed most was the feeling of the carbon monoxide in his mouth and on the back of his throat as he inhaled. He still remembers it so well.

There's a feeling of drinking a can of soda. The carbonated liquid tingles on the back of your throat. It's similar. As a result, he drank between four and eight club sodas a day, and he bought three to four cases of carbonated water a week.

What he did not get was the feeling of smoke going into his lungs. The warmth—the fire-breathing. And there was nothing that could replace it. No electronic cigarette, no nicotine replacement drug. Smoking was smoking, and it was *impossible* to explain the love/hate relationship, the pleasure/pain relationship a smoker experienced with the product. It actually was fire-breathing, and it was one of the most pleasurable pastimes on this earth. He would do it all day long if it wasn't so fucking bad for him.

The ultimate effects are still unknown at the time of use of this very special product. Had anybody ever smoked a cigarette and had a stroke right then and there? In all his years in the industry, he'd never heard of that happening. It was sustained, long-term use of the product that would cause it to happen.

It was a game, and it was a gamble. Ultimately, you were gambling with your life.

He knew it was a gamble thanks to Dr. Richard Doll and his research into the smoking habits of thousands of British doctors.

It turned out the incredible Dr. Doll had kept up with his fire-breathing doctors.

For five decades, Doll followed up with the group, and thereby learned more than anyone else ever had about the effects that a lifetime of smoking had on humans. The good doctor released several reports based on this long arc of smoking research.

In fact, fifty years after Doll published his first report, he and his colleagues published a grand finale to the series, just months before his own death, in 2005. By then, he'd been knighted by the Queen for his distinguished career at Oxford University, where a new building was constructed with his name on it, and which opened shortly after he died.

Here's some of the very bad news Doll had uncovered over a lifetime of corresponding with the group of British doctors who smoked.

Half of those doctors died of smoking-related diseases; and half of those deaths were in middle age. Basically, one in two smokers died of smoking. And it wasn't just from lung cancer; more than twenty fatal diseases were causally linked to cigarette smoking. Cigarettes killed you, they could kill you in middle age, and death from smoking could arrive in varied and horrible ways.

However, there was positive news as well, and it was that positive news from Doll's later findings that led the lawyer to give up smoking on his parents' back porch.

The positive news was this.

According to Doll and the cohort of smoking doctors he followed, there existed a best-before age for giving up the habit and living a healthy life.

Doll discovered that people who gave up smoking at thirty-five years of age—or before—had a chance to essentially repair their physical body. If they stopped smoking by that age, their body could return to a health and purity level within 98 percent of what it was before they started smoking, thereby giving them no more chance of having a heart attack or getting lung cancer than a non-smoker had.

Now that was powerful data.

What Doll's research also revealed was that although thirty-five seemed to be the best-before age, it was never too late to give up smoking and receive positive effects.

According to his study, the average heavy smoker lost eleven years of their life if they kept it up until the end. But if you gave it up at fifty, you received years back. And if you gave it up at seventy, you received years back.

The health benefits were immediate, and applicable to everyone, no matter how long they'd smoked.

When Doll's final report came out, the US surgeon general didn't take the same energy to publicize Doll's most current findings, nor did any tobacco company. Why didn't the surgeon general or big tobacco run with this news?

———

Well, it seems pretty obvious.

The tobacco companies didn't want to highlight it because the findings showed that the effects of their product were even worse than everyone thought. The health authorities didn't want to highlight the research either, because it could be interpreted as saying it was safe to smoke until you were thirty-five years old, by which time you could be addicted and unable to give up easily.

That didn't discourage the lawyer. He had followed Doll's research for years.

After all, it was Doll and the surgeon general who were largely responsible for his own career in Big Tobacco. Virtually every tobacco law or restriction that was passed had been justified on the grounds of health research, which ultimately originated with the surgeon general's report and Dr. Doll's findings. This time, the lawyer decided to listen.

He was thirty-seven years old when he decided to quit—just two years past Doll's best-before date. And now he wanted those eleven years back. So, he decided to take them. And once he decided to take them, he wasn't prepared to give them up. And to this day, that's what stops him from smoking.

The painful gnawing of withdrawal goes away eventually. For him, it went away within a few months. Once the nicotine withdrawal symptoms had gone, it didn't end, though, unfortunately.

He still had cravings. The strong memories of emotional and pleasurable aspects of smoking never went away. He still missed the tingling on the back of his throat, the satisfaction of smoking after a meal. The feeling of wanting to be fire-breathing never left, that was the truth.

As the years went by, he thought about it less and less, though. He did still think about it, however, and once or twice a year he was tempted. In those moments of temptation, he thought about those eleven years, and he was not prepared to give them back.

He took Doll's deal, and that's what stopped him every time he was tempted to have a cigarette. Having a disapproving wife and two children didn't hurt either. To be honest, his wife and kids made all the difference. He loved them, and he wanted to be there for them as long as he could.

Without love, couldn't life dissolve into slow suicide? Maybe, ultimately, that was what smoking was. It sounded corny, but he chose love, and he was determined to honour this new vow: never smoke again.

In Canada, something unique occurred that has never, so far as the lawyer knew, happened anywhere else on the planet.

It had started in Quebec, way back circa 1998—the same year the Master Settlement Agreement was worked out in the US—when two class-action lawsuits were launched on behalf of thousands of smokers in that province.

It took more than twenty years to play out, but eventually those suits led to a damning result for Canadian tobacco companies. In 2015, a Quebec judge ruled in favour of the smokers, who'd been struck with severe health conditions—throat cancer, heart disease, emphysema—or early death. His Honour, in return, struck the Three Smokes with a substantial bill of almost $16 billion in moral and punitive damages. They launched an appeal, of course.

By that point, the Canadian federal government had completely obliterated the images of specific tobacco brands: all cigarette packs were now uniform, no matter the brand. Their colour was brown, and most of the package was a horrible-looking graphic health warning. Basically, the only detail that told a smoker which brand they were buying was its name printed in uniform font beneath the health warning.

In the meantime, all the Canadian provinces had decided to sue the Three Smokes to recover health care costs incurred because of smoking-related illnesses over the decades, and now it looked as if those provinces could actually win.

Quebec alone was asking for $61 billion, while Ontario was asking for much more: $330 billion. In total, the amount of money being demanded from the Three Smokes by the provinces, along with the Quebec civil suits, was in the ballpark of $500 billion. This figure was far in excess of the $200 billion Big Tobacco had agreed to pay south of the border.

In 2019, after their appeal in the Quebec class-action suit failed, the Three Smokes immediately sought creditor protection, and when it was granted, all tobacco-related lawsuits in Canada were paused. The industry and government representatives agreed to sit down together in a quiet back room (far away from a public court-room) to try to come up with the big number owing. Sound familiar? What would that figure be?

The lawyer watched this epic legal battle with great interest.

He was fascinated that no other industry had come to the defence of the Three Smokes. After all, the assault by the Canadian government and its provinces on this one particular industry had been with the aim to win at all costs, as far as he could tell. When existing laws weren't effective, the governments simply changed them. When British Columbia launched its first lawsuit, the province lost. So the province simply passed a new law, refiled its lawsuit, and—no surprise—won. Was that democratic? It was a razor's edge. The lawyer saw what was happening as the ultimate bureaucratic wokeness, but the result had the potential of leading to a revolutionary scenario.

Maybe Canada would be the first country in the world to bankrupt its cigarette industry and therefore to end its tobacco paradox.

If it could happen at all, the lawyer believed it would happen here in Canada, one of the undisputed global leaders in anti-tobacco strategies.

Still, that extreme ending was doubtful—based on, well, the entire history of capitalism thus far. Don't hold your breath, thought the lawyer.

HIDING IN THE OPEN

One afternoon, a few years after he had quit, the lawyer brought home a gift for one of his daughters. It was a package of glossy stickers of famous brand designs from all over the world.

These were iconic global logos: Coca-Cola, Nike, Ferrari.

He watched with pleasure as she opened the package and spread out all those familiar logos across the floor, examining them, moving them around, and proudly pointing out to him what each of them represented. She knew most of them.

When her eyes landed on the Marlboro sticker, she picked up the white rooftop-shaped logo on its shiny red background and held it up in front of her father.

"What's this one, Daddy?" she asked.

His daughter had no idea what the logo was or which product it was affiliated with.

It was a marvel for him to witness. He stared dumbfounded at his young daughter, who was looking up at him, holding the sticker in her little hand.

He didn't know if he should even tell her what the simple image represented.

In late 2019, the CEO of Philip Morris International, maker of the mighty Marlboro, gave a series of interviews to major media outlets in which he announced that he and his company hoped smokers would stop smoking.

Philip Morris was looking ahead and dreamed of a "smokeless future," he stated. This was surprising, to say the least. It was as if the CEO was acknowledging that his company was caught in the never-ending tobacco paradox and wanted a way out.

In one interview, on BBC News *Hardtalk*, that CEO was eviscerated by the show's host, who demanded to know why the industry hadn't simply shut itself down. Wouldn't closing up shop be the best way to dissuade smokers from continuing to smoke? Wouldn't it be the right thing to do? The host was enraged.

The CEO was selling a new product that had been years in the making. It was Philip Morris's version of the holy grail: a "safer" cigarette, in which, instead of tobacco being burned, it was simply heated—addictive mist instead of smoke.

Vaping and heated tobacco had become the new frontier for nicotine delivery, and even as the tobacco wars continued, R & D departments worked diligently to invent new offerings that were more socially palatable, as well as profitable.

It's truly incredible to consider that Philip Morris was still ranked in the Fortune 250 club, more than fifty years after the surgeon general officially announced that cigarettes were linked to lung cancer and to early, painful death. As you've learned, most international tobacco companies are still doing quite well, in fact.

Even though the wealthiest segment of society gave up smoking en masse starting in the 1980s, the apparatus that protects the world's economic elite remains committed to cigarettes: investment advisers, financial institutions, and trillion-dollar retirement funds still enjoy the generous profit margins generated from the business of Jill and Joe Smoker.

Anyone who desires more context need only look up Dr. Bronwyn King. The Australian radiation oncologist discovered that the pension plan she and fellow hospital employees—including droves of doctors—were contributing to was heavily invested in Big Tobacco stocks. Her response: she is now the CEO of a company seeking to eliminate tobacco stocks from global investment portfolios, a Herculean task, it turns out.

The reality is that industries with happy customers are simply not designed to be shut down, ever; corporations are designed only to deliver profits to their shareholders, with almost no exceptions. In that sense, tobacco has become the leading contemporary example of the icy stakes of capitalism, and so the tobacco paradox continues to unfold.

The cigarette has become the most peculiar and outrageous fast-moving consumer good that has ever been mass produced.

It is certainly also the deadliest popular product ever invented by humans for humans to use—after all, it is the one product that, when used as intended, is harmful, and potentially deadly, to the individual who uses it.

For this reason, it really is "special." A dangerous consumer anomaly.

Of course, if cigarettes were invented today, this addictive and deadly product would never be allowed into the consumer marketplace, and would certainly not be for sale at your corner store.

And let's be clear, it is shocking that it's still available on the corner, because no matter what any government's anti-smoking strategy is, or how much money is thrown into warning the consumer, if a product is available at your corner store, your conclusion will ultimately be this: How bad could a cigarette really be for me if it's for sale with bubble gum and chocolate bars?

Given the powerful addictive properties of nicotine—a drug—there is really only one logical place where this product should be stocked, where drugs are monitored and dispensed by trained medical professionals: at neighbourhood pharmacies.

Regardless of where they are sold, trillions of sticks are still being sold each year; governments are still making strides and proclaiming victories in the war against smoking; and tobacco companies are continuing to earn massive profits.

Meanwhile, most people believe that the debate over cigarettes has come and gone and that Big Tobacco lost—even as companies continue to win and consolidate into more-powerful global empires.

Case in point, Reynolds American bought one-hit-menthol-wonder Lorillard in 2015 for $27 billion. Later that year, Japan Tobacco International acquired the international business of Natural American—the file which the lawyer had helped grow—from Reynolds for an impressive $5 billion. In 2017, British American Tobacco bought a piece of Tobacco Road, acquiring Reynolds American for almost $50 billion. Now that's confidence.

Even with the tidal waves of anti-smoking campaigns and government legislation rolling across the planet, human population growth means there are now more smokers—not fewer—than at any time in history: of the 7.8 billion people on Earth, over 1 billion of them smoke.

It's been more than half a millennium since tobacco was first introduced to Europe.

And five hundred plus years ago, there was another Drake who became really famous, but he wasn't a singer, he was a sailor, circa the mid-1500s.

Francis Drake was a fearsome English pirate to any Spanish vessel he came across. Drake spent most of his adult life on the ocean, where he became adept at pillaging Spanish gold, burning Spanish ships, and generally wreaking havoc on that enemy colonial naval power, which nicknamed him El Draque, "The Dragon."

Drake was the son of a farmer, but he ran away from home when young and earned his sea legs on the fleet operated by a family of sea merchants called Hawkins, who blurred the line between colonial commerce and piracy.

It was John Hawkins, a mentor and cousin to Drake, who was the first Englishman to bring tobacco home to England, after a voyage to South America in 1565. A few years later, Drake brought some back too.

The Hawkins clan taught Drake the basics of morally dubious, ocean-faring economics; he was soon involved in illegally shipping enslaved Africans to the Spanish colonies in the West Indies and became commander of a vessel by the time he was just twenty-five years old: a young pirate-merchant of the Caribbean.

Drake's battles with the Spanish fleet were vicious, and he often emerged victorious. The Dragon had a knack for the pirate life, and his daring on the waves caught the attention of the English monarch, Queen Elizabeth.

After all, England didn't honour the Spanish claim to South America, and the queen appreciated Drake's enterprising manner; in him she spied an opportunity to disrupt her colonial adversaries. To help Drake along, she gave him something that any pirate could only dream of: an official privateering commission, a royal licence to plunder and maim Spanish interests. It was an early, saltier version of Her Majesty's Secret Service, and Drake carried out his mission of destruction with pleasure.

The queen's Dragon went on to explore other oceans too. Drake was the first English sailor to cross America and reach the Pacific, and the first to circumnavigate the globe. Along the way he delivered pain to any Spanish vessel or outpost he encountered, with her majesty's glowing approval.

When Drake made it home two years later, with heaps of plundered treasure and spices, he was knighted by Elizabeth on the deck of his ship. He'd become a pirate-lord, and the title of "Sir" was added to his trove of prizes.

To the Spanish Armada, Drake was a wretched criminal—a thief and a murderer—but he was, in fact, operating with the official support and protection of the government of his day. He was both a pirate and a government agent, and it was this duality which propelled him forward to explore far-off lands, and to make himself rich beyond his dreams.

Pirates aren't always what they seem. Sometimes they are supported by and work in the service of the government—perceived outlaws who, in fact, serve the laws of their lands, or seas.

There is no industry in the ecosystem of consumer goods that could withstand the level of punishment the tobacco industry has incurred without the benefit of similar government alliance and protection.

The tobacco industry has managed to navigate and survive an intense decades-long war on its products by the medical establishment and by governments from around the world only because it has also been aided, and protected from this assault, by those very same governments: this double-dealing by the "house" is the source of the tobacco paradox.

The motive? Follow the money, as the old and trusted adage goes.

The revenues that governments enjoy from the sale of tobacco remain staggering: the UK's average annual revenue from taxation of tobacco products is £12 billion. In the US, tobacco taxes account for about $12 billion a year, and that doesn't include the MSA payments delivered to the individual US states as part of the Master Settlement Agreement.

Is it fair to ask whether Western governments are addicted to tobacco revenues?

The numbers speak for themselves.

Still, a handful of countries are actively seeking ways to end the paradox. Canada is finding out if it's possible to sue tobacco companies into corporate oblivion. If those suits are successful, what would that mean for Canadian smokers? Where would those who are already hooked procure their supply? Smokers always find a way.

New Zealand, another leader in anti-tobacco strategies, came up with a different approach, which could offer a solution to the Canadians should their industry be bankrupted.

In December 2021, the government of New Zealand announced that it will end the sale of tobacco to anyone born after 2008. So they are allowing those already addicted to continue fire-breathing, but the next generation is off limits to tobacco companies. It's an intriguing solution, as well as a tempting scenario for any enterprising black-market pirate in the region.

Meanwhile, it took almost 20 years, but in 2022 Switzerland did vote to ban tobacco advertising, although it still hasn't ratified the WHO Framework Convention on Tobacco Control, even as 181 other countries have done so, a treaty which the United States has never signed.

Remember Bhutan, the tiny, predominantly Buddhist country in the Eastern Himalayas that outlawed smoking as early as 1729? It remains committed to keeping tobacco away—just one part of the country's "Gross National Happiness" strategy. The sale of cigarettes is banned in most of its districts—though tourists can still buy cigarettes—and it boasts the lowest national smoking rate in the world at about 1 percent.

For now, Bhutan is singular, the only nation not caught in the tobacco paradox.

To smoke a cigarette remains for the time being a legal adult choice in almost every country in the world—one you are free to make despite all of the medical evidence that shows just how harmful smoking is to the human body. Almost every smoker understands this particular paradox all too well: it's really bad for you, but it feels so good.

You can give up smoking, though—and worldwide about one and a half million people do stop each year. If you happen to smoke, think about Richard Doll's findings. He was knighted by the Queen for a reason. How many lives has his groundbreaking research saved thus far? It's unknown, but probably tens of millions and counting. If you're a smoker, there's still time for you to get a few years back, should you choose.

The Legend, unfortunately, was not one of those. The New York–born, Jewish Southern lawyer smoked until the day he died. At sixty-nine years old, he suffered a heart attack as he was leaving the gym.

There is no question that from the moment Dr. Doll discovered the link between lung cancer and cigarettes, the industry titans fought back, through alternate facts and disinformation, through sophisticated marketing and public relations campaigns, through legal manoeuvring as well as illegal and immoral tactics. This has been well documented and reported over decades.

What's fascinating is that the lawyer's journey—as he rose through the industry and travelled the world—did not lead him to the same conclusions about the tobacco industry that are popularly held by others.

On his corporate odyssey through this contentious global industry, after all, it was his job to make sure his employer was compliant with government rules as they shifted and tightened. And he always did comply. It took him years to understand that the very governments that he first viewed as being adversaries were also acting as allies at the same time—like that ancient symbol of a snake consuming its own tail.

And in all of those years, he had never seen a pack of cigarettes sold out of a gym bag in front of a high school, or been coerced into breaking the marketing or advertising rules in any country he was patrolling on behalf of the company. Maybe this was the result simply of the high level of scrutiny and attention being applied to the industry by the time he was recruited in 2001. The level of corporate responsibility the companies he worked for were required to show, and the onerous laws and burden of compliance he had to work under, were extraordinary, and he maintains that he was never once asked to do anything illegal.

The lawyer's career is a sort of Rorschach test: how you view and judge his professional trajectory probably reveals how you feel about the systems and forces that rule our world. For some, his corporate journey may bring to mind the concept of the banality of evil, while others may simply view it as business as usual. If every company or corporation had the same scrutiny applied to it as the tobacco industry has had, would the capitalistic machine we are all part of be improved?

Of course, this may sound crazy when describing an industry that has been single-handily responsible for hundreds of millions of otherwise preventable deaths and unimaginable pain and suffering —and will continue to inflict pain and suffering upon so many.

The very process of keeping this product easily available on the legal market has strained the very boundaries of capitalism in so many countries—and its survival is proof that in our fast-moving, entrepreneurial world, we're willing to innovate almost anything, it seems, except the system of capitalism itself.

Ultimately, wherever in the world they may live, no matter their economic circumstances, those who smoke for a lifetime have a good chance of enduring a truly unhappy ending.

Cigarettes, literally and then figuratively, break our hearts.

FYI, there's no such thing as an international lawyer.

Lawyers practise by jurisdiction, and although he was now living in Canada, he was certainly not qualified to practise law there. So, what next . . . another pirate ship?

Well, there were certain advantages to having entered such a contentious global industry as legal counsel at twenty-six years of age.

Most of the people who exited the tobacco industry with the kind of knowledge and experience that he had amassed were actually heading out to golden pastures—retiring completely from corporate life: playing golf, travelling in style, spoiling their grandchildren—spending some of the treasure they'd earned over the course of a lucrative career.

But he was far too young for that. The lawyer still had much of his professional career ahead of him, he hoped.

Once a person has served at the highest levels of the corporate world and travelled to so many countries in that service, there's a name for what comes next: "consultant."

It turned out there were a lot of companies operating in grey-area industries, and they wanted to know what he had learned about how the world worked, and how to apply those lessons to their own products and services.

Over the course of the next few years, he set up a management consultant company which specialized in legal and business development issues. He took on clients all over the United States, the UK, and even in Switzerland.

And contentious industries came calling: cannabis, gambling, and online betting. He picked up work for travel service companies as well; and, yes, he was even approached by an investor who was exploring the acquisition of one of the most famous pornography magazines in the world. It reminded the lawyer of way back when he and Leah were in their cramped office guessing which contentious industry Heather the headhunter was representing.

He also enjoyed the challenges of serving on the board of directors for a start-up company producing magic-mushroom edibles. He'd thought psychedelics had come and gone, but old drugs in new packaging were trending: cures for familiar anxieties or gateways to spiritual journeys. It was kind of trippy—he'd sampled the product, of course—and business was booming. Or shrooming.

Thankfully, he still had the chance to travel for business.

One drawback to building his own consultancy, though, was that there was no more corporate expense account. When it came to booking air travel, for example, he'd had to give up his business-class habits. Now that those expenses were coming out of his own pocket, he was sitting at the back of the plane in economy, pretending to read the airline magazine or browsing new releases, waiting for the drink cart.

Sometimes, if he was on an aisle, he might space out and watch the curtain towards the front of the cabin open and close as flight attendants passed through, knowing in precise detail exactly what was happening on the other side, even if he was no longer considered a member of that VIP club.

Believe it or not, after all those air miles earned, he still found it thrilling to buckle up and feel the turbo speed of the heavy aircraft as it accelerated on the runway, all that trembling and shaking. Was it his imagination, or was it a bumpier ride back here, outside the protection of the corporate bubble?

Then came that wonderful moment when the wheels lifted off the ground and the calming sound of clean, filtered air rushed out of the ventilation system into nervous lungs. If there was turbulence on the way up to cruising altitude, a lot of eyes were focused on the lit-up seatbelt signs, as if staring at them hard enough would make them blink off.

He was more likely to smile at the No Smoking symbol, glowing right beside the seatbelt sign. He liked to imagine it would blink off as well, but, of course, smoking had been banned on airplanes almost thirty years ago—a generation.

Advertising cigarettes may now be illegal in most Western consumer markets, but there is one ingenious way smoking is still advertised, and everywhere—to the broadest possible audience, and free of charge to the industry.

It is probably the simplest and most effective advertising campaign for a consumer product ever executed. It is uniform and universal, transcending language and culture, and it appears in public spaces and waiting areas, outside of soaring office buildings, in five-star and one-star hotels, bars, pubs, movie theatre lobbies, cafés, and art galleries, on trains, buses, and airplanes—and across the world.

It's devastatingly simple: a symbol of a platonic cigarette encircled with a red line, with another red line that cuts diagonally across the floating black stick.

No Smoking.

It's a reminder to anyone: you *can't* smoke here, but you *can* smoke.

Most companies could never envision an ad campaign in which their product would be marketed free of charge, at eye level, in every public square, in every city, and, indeed, above every city to every passenger on an airplane—whether they went economy or first class, whether they used the product or not.

Can you imagine how much money a company would have to pay to rent space in every major venue across the world, indoors and outside, to advertise one product? A truly global ad campaign which is hiding in the open. No company could afford the price.

Smoking is still an option: that's the message every No Smoking sign delivers. It's just not an option at this particular moment, in this particular place.

Perhaps, in the future, when those millions of No Smoking signs are removed, we will know, finally, that smoking is no longer possible. It simply won't be on our minds.

For now, smoking is always just around the corner on a convenience store shelf, even if in many countries it's behind a metal cabinet door or underneath the counter—a secret club, just behind the curtain.

Even now sometimes, on a flight just after takeoff, the captain or cabin director, making routine announcements over the PA system, will remind passengers that smoking is not permitted in the airplane cabin or in the washrooms. It's as if they were reading aloud the rules of an old game, telling their captive audience what it already knows, with everyone quietly playing along.

By then, of course, most passengers are already plugged into their inflight entertainment, browsing movie and episodic TV titles—hoping to kill some flying time while absorbing one of the world's oldest and most popular consumer recipes, one on which we are all dependent: a good story with a happy ending.

ACKNOWLEDGMENTS

Thank you to my agent, Samantha Haywood, and the incredible team at Transatlantic Agency for their guidance, support, and for the energy and nerve required to help transform an idea into a book.

Thank you to the lawyer, his wife, and their family, for their patience and a continued conversation which lasted a decade.

Thank you to Alanna McMullen, the intrepid editor who made this project a dream to work on, and the exceptional team at Penguin Canada, including Penguin Canada's publisher Nicole Winstanley; publicity and marketing managers Dan French and Stephen Myers; and cover designer Dylan Browne. And to Diane Turbide, the acquiring editor who made this experience possible. Thanks to copy editor Alex Schultz and proofreader Crissy Calhoun.

These generous souls provided valuable ideas, insights, edits, or constructive feedback on various drafts: Jess Gibson, Judith Knelman, Graham Roumieu, Meg Storey, Norman Wright, Jeff Parker, Jane Warren, Daniel Weinzweig, Rachel Harry, Martha Haldenby, Rachel Giese, Martyn Burke, Douglas Knight, Andrew

Westoll, Hilary Doyle, Daniel Goldbloom, Antonio de Luca, Richard Stursberg, Jason Logan, Bernard Schiff, Christopher Flavelle, Garvia Bailey, Richard Poplak, Jack Shapiro, and Margaret Atwood.

Thank you to my peers and instructors at Banff Centre for Arts and Creativity's Literary Journalism program; in 2012 they helped shape a creative non-fiction longform piece which evolved into this book project. And thank you to the amazing crew at Banff Centre who, during my time there, helped me along the way, including Janice Price, Rosemary Thompson, Joel Ivany, Meg Power, Marie-Helene Dagenais, Jennifer Knorr, Erin Brandt Filliter, Kyla Jacobs, Ryan McIntosh, Nicky "another-day-another-dollar" Lynch, and Jim Olver.

For support and good cheer, thank you to my partner Nicole and my family: Bernadette, Martin, Sara, Mark, and Leo; John and Martine; and Jonathan, Rachel, Daniel, and Josh. And to Joel, Mark, Ashley, and Kaia.

And, thanks to you, the reader, for spending time with these pages.